4i LEADERSHIP

Interrupt : Imagine : Ignite : Impact

Start a bolder conversation

ANTHONY LANDALE & IAN LOCK

Praise for 4i Leadership

"Practical, exciting and bold, 4i Leadership is essential reading for any aspiring or practising leader."
Stuart Crainer, co-founder, Thinkers50

"I really loved reading this book and found it so empowering. We have been lucky enough to work with Ian and the team this year and have benefited hugely from exploring 4i Leadership with our leaders and putting these techniques into practice during an extensive change period."
Helen Milford, Director of Retail, Sainsbury's Argos

"This book is easy to read and simple to understand. If you are not lucky enough to have Ian or Anthony as a coach then read this book. It certainly helped me be a much better version of myself."
Monique Carter, Global SVP People and Organisation, Novo Nordisk

"I was very impressed how this leadership methodology influenced my management team. Although being a very diverse, multinational team it enabled us to make a big impact on communication and cooperation within a very short time."
Josef Guggenhuber, member of the supervisory board, Symbion AG

"For anyone who has leadership ambitions, Ian and Anthony will encourage you to have forward-looking conversations about your own leadership, empowering you to own your individual success."
Meredith Pierce-Hunter, Director, Kew Foundation, Royal Botanic Gardens, Kew

"These guys totally demystify the subject of leadership. As a leader in a complex organisation I experienced some amazing results by using their techniques. My advice is ... have those bolder conversations, focus on building trust, and above all, make the future exciting for you and your teams!"
Stephen Beresford, Head of Marketing, REHAU

"This book is an engaging and truly thought provoking read which had me reflecting on and challenging my own leadership throughout. Reading this book is like having your own personal coach in the room with you. A must read for any leader who is wanting to build a high performing culture."
Debbie Smith, CEO Retail, The Post Office

"I loved this book – a great read with practical examples to get you thinking about your own leadership context."
Susie Balch, Vice Dean, Advancement, London Business School

"I've had the great privilege of learning to lead more authentically by working with Ian over a number of years – It's wonderful to see him and Anthony put their practice onto paper in this gem of a book."

Emma Woods, CEO, Wagamama

"4I Leadership will influence your thinking. If you want to be surrounded by people who bring energy to your work and create a possibility mindset, then read this book! The unique insights within it can last forever."

Ekkehard Köhler, CEO, Bleistahl Group

"Comprehensive in its range, 4i Leadership is an intelligent and insightful book about the essential foundations of leadership. It exposes the power of mixing deep conversations with empowering beliefs, and the impact one can then have on people."

Stéphane Jacqmin, Head of Consumer Healthcare, Turkey, Middle-East and China, SANOFI Consumer Healthcare

---

"The 4i approach is a simple but powerful way to help leaders answer the challenges of modern leadership. Whether you pick this book up as a standalone tool to support your own development or to help support change in your wider organisation, I'd challenge even the most seasoned leader not to find value in this approach."

Madeline Shaw, Marketing Director, Boots Opticians

"Working with Anthony was a joy. I went deeper into the "why" of my leadership than I had ever done before and re-examined everything in my life and work. It was rewarding, stimulating and brilliantly challenging. A new, unexpected, and incredibly exciting direction emerged. 4i Leadership can be truly life-changing!"

Kate Barker, Independent Brand Consultant

"Anthony and Ian continue to inspire leadership insight and practice with a brilliant simplicity and relevance that just works. 4i Leadership will change your leadership and your life!"

Sue Burrows, Former CIO

"Quite simply the best insight into practical leadership skills development I've ever come across. If you are at all curious about leadership, then have the courage to read and digest the invaluable learnings in this book."

Chris Welham, CEO, Wadworth

4i Leadership

Interrupt : Imagine : Ignite : Impact

Start a bolder conversation

www.4ileader.com

First published in Great Britain 2019

Design by www.jebensdesign.co.uk

ISBN:

978-1-5272-4157-2

A huge thank you

This book would not have been written without the care and commitment of some very special people. First of all a big thank you to our families and especially to Margaret and Diane, for their patience and forbearance as we shaped this book, many times over.

Thanks also to our friends and colleagues:

- First and foremost to Anni Townend for her invaluable input, inspiration and early editing that helped us set off in the right direction. Also for being such a committed and courageous partner over so many years.
- Emily Day, John Pringle and Martin Carter for their joyful collaboration and encouragement. They, alongside Anni, are a wonderful team we are privileged to be part of.
- Steve Radcliffe whose leadership work with Future Engage Deliver has been our bedrock and inspiration for so many years.
- Also to our friends and clients – especially Ekkehard Köhler, Susie Balch, Simon Roberts and Jonathan Gardner who generously offered to be beta readers as we got close to the end of our writing.
- Also the many hundreds of clients and thousands of leaders we've worked with over the past 20 years who have not only helped us learn so many valuable lessons but who have also provided great feedback that kept us grounded.
- And not forgetting Stuart Crainer, editor extraordinaire, whose final touch helped us get this book over the line. And Viki Jebens whose design lifted the words from the page and made what we'd imagined look better than we ever expected.

CONTENTS

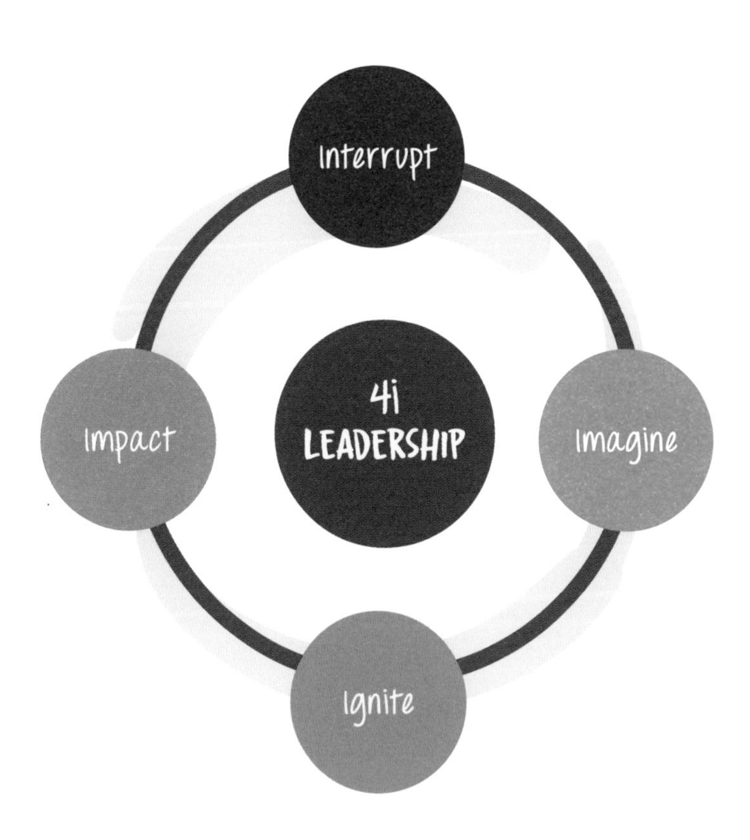
Interrupt
4i
LEADERSHIP
Impact
Imagine
Ignite

For over 20 years we've been helping people to revolutionise their leadership. We've worked with leaders and teams in organisations across the world as well as with individuals in local communities. We've worked with teachers, retailers, engineers and fundraisers as well as entrepreneurs, civil servants and volunteers. We've hosted major conferences, run thousands of workshops and coached people from every walk of life. And we've witnessed first-hand the inspiring breakthroughs that many we have worked with have made.

In writing this book we wanted to stimulate the same appetite and sense of excitement that we have experienced working with individual leaders and teams. And we want to help you become a more powerful leader by starting a bolder conversation with you. One where you feel invited to join in. One where there are as many questions as answers. And one you thoroughly enjoy.

In simple terms, here's what this book is all about:

- **Interrupt:** when you notice that things are stuck or moving too slowly you have to be willing to challenge what's going on
- **Imagine:** but you also need a dream of something that could be much better
- **Ignite:** and most of the time you will need to bring other people along with you
- **Impact:** so that together you can make the difference you want

These are, we believe, the essential foundations for your leadership, and in the following pages we will bring 4i Leadership to life so you can explore what it means for you.

Anthony Landale and Ian Lock

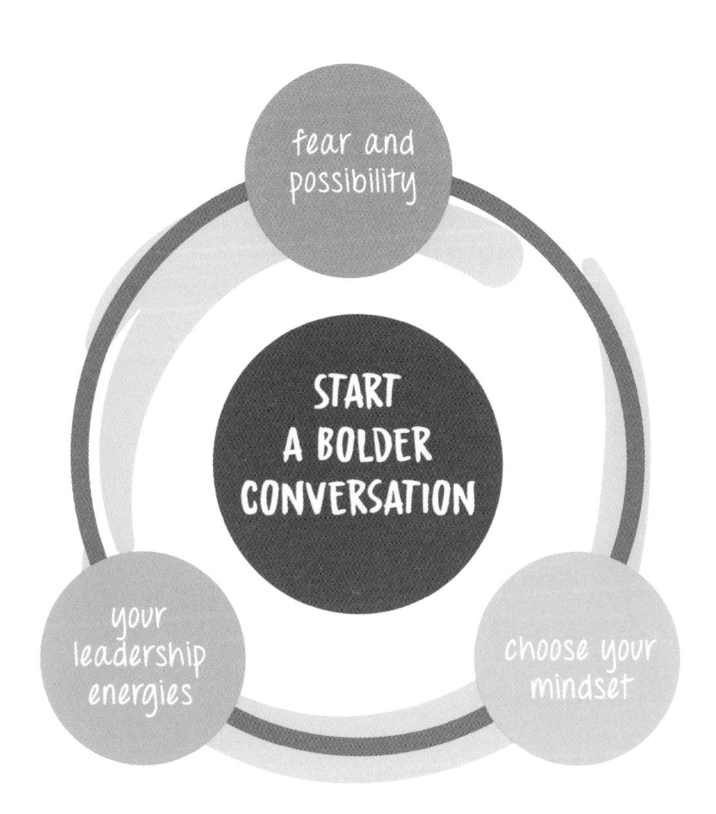
fear and possibility
START A BOLDER CONVERSATION
your leadership energies
choose your mindset

Start a bolder conversation

Be brave enough to start a conversation that matters ... and keep it going!

Bolder conversations sit at the heart of 4i Leadership. For us this is the ability to have robust and courageous exchanges that are inspired by possibility rather than driven by fear. Conversations like these bring more focus and creativity to our endeavours. They also embrace challenge and invitation, attentive listening and deep enquiry. With this in mind take note, bolder conversations may be enlivening but they aren't necessarily easy or comfortable.

As you read on, the first place to start such a conversation is with yourself. We will provide stories, questions and enquiries that we ask you to match with your interest, energy and commitment. And whether you have 40 years' experience or you are just starting out as a leader doesn't matter. We encourage you to take whatever resonates with you, share your thoughts with someone who supports you and clarify with them how you want to take this conversation forward.

You may find it useful to apply the real world scenarios you are dealing with to the material that you read. Notice how you react to what you enjoy and what really annoys you. All your reactions are worth paying attention to as they contain valuable information. If you pause for a moment and look a bit deeper there might well be something useful there.

Most importantly, however, we believe that your 4i journey and the bolder conversations you initiate can open up breakthrough possibilities for you.

So take the 4i approach and use it to engage in those conversations that will accelerate your leadership. The personal and business clients that we've worked with have found that 4i gives them a simple flow as well as a practical platform from which to develop new insights and create real value. Also, for any meaningful conversation, listening is as important as speaking and in the following section we've highlighted what you need to bring.

Intentional listening

A conversation without listening is like a car without a road – it has nowhere to go.

To be in a conversation that opens up possibilities, listen intently and for what you don't already know. Here are five principles to get you started.

1 **Notice what matters** When you are attentive in your listening you will notice that people always talk about what matters to them. You can hear this not only in the words but in the tone, the volume and the topics they are choosing to focus on.

2 **Notice what's missing** What's missing in a conversation can be surprisingly revealing. For example, what do we notice when people are silent? What do we learn from the things that they don't talk about?

3 **Notice what's shaping your listening** Notice your beliefs, assumptions and preconceptions and don't let them get in the way of what the other person is saying.

4 **Notice your inner chatter** There are two obstacles that often get in the way when we're listening to other people – wanting to look good and wanting to be right. Notice that when you're driven by this inner voice you won't be listening to anyone. Instead you will be waiting to jump in and give your opinion.

5 **Listen with anticipation** This shows up in the way you're breathing, in your eye contact and in the absence of your judgement. When we are attentive in our listening there is a generosity of spirit. We are interested in what they might be about to say and we create a space for anything to emerge.

In this respect 4i will help you to look at where you may need to pay more attention and bring more intent. Much of our work with leaders over the years has been about combining the right conversation with the ability to be curious. To help us start this conversation here are two underpinning ideas we want to explore. These ideas weave throughout the 4i approach and will help you engage with any of the leadership issues you may be facing. They are:

1. How to bring a possibility mindset to your leadership
2. How to use your energy as a leadership resource

Fear and possibility

Are you driven by fear or inspired by possibility?

This has been one of our favourite questions over the years. It allows us to understand how our mindset drives our behaviour.

Mindset is about our attitude and beliefs. It is our mindset that deeply affects the way we engage with life. Just think of people who are always optimistic or pessimistic and you can immediately see one way in which mindset influences us. But what makes people choose one attitude over the other? What do they get out of choosing the one they have? And how easy is it for them to choose differently?

Over the years we have met many people who are driven – ourselves included. And while many of us are driven by success, that drive can be influenced by two opposing mindsets that we call the fearful mindset and the possibility mindset. Let's look at how these support or undermine the results you want to achieve as a leader.

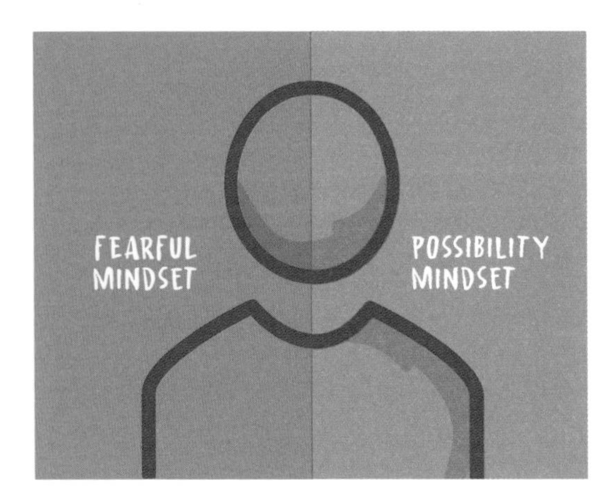

The fearful mindset

Everything you want is on the other side of fear – Jack Canfield

A fearful mindset is characterised by anxiety, fixed thinking and often a sense that it's not our fault. We can feel defensive and expect the worst. The following story typifies the fearful mindset and it's a story we hear a lot.

When we met Sophie she was an ambitious manager in a fast moving retail business. As she talked through her issues it quickly became apparent what mindset she was in. For Sophie, there were winners and losers and she was desperate to win. But more than this she constantly needed to prove herself and when she spoke about some of the difficult situations she found herself in, none of them were her fault. People didn't understand her customers. She hadn't been getting the right support from HR. She didn't have time to talk to and understand her people.

Sophie wasn't easy to coach. To start with she seemed to have little appetite for learning and although she wanted success she seemed to want it mostly in order to boost her own self-esteem.

Sophie was being driven by fear. She evaluated everything in her life by the results she achieved. If her performance figures were good then she felt better about herself, at least temporarily. When results weren't so good she became brittle and defensive. And her response to any challenge was to withdraw.

This was frustrating for Sophie's peers but the impact she was having on her own team was even worse. The expectations she had of her direct reports were impossibly high and she judged success in very black and white terms. She praised her people when they were hitting their targets but criticised them when they weren't. As a result her team were fixated on the short term, they were anxious much of the time and they never took any risks in case they became the target for Sophie's ire.

Sophie of course couldn't see that she needed help and any suggestion that she did triggered reactive behaviour. She felt let down. She blamed others. She quickly got angry.

Many of us have similar responses when we are facing difficulties and we find it hard to let others in. 'I'm my own harshest critic', Sophie said. But that was more of the same problem. Sophie related to help as an admission of failure. In her mind it was losers that needed help. Winners delivered results with little effort. And she was fearful that by accepting coaching she would be admitting to her own deep sense of inadequacy.

The possibility mindset

Because you are alive everything is possible – Thich Nhat Hahn

A possibility mindset is characterised by a sense that we can make anything happen. It's all within our reach and all obstacles are there to be overcome.

You may have noticed how refreshing it is to work with people who are coachable, people who know that they don't have all the answers and who invite curiosity and new insights. Such people often have a possibility mindset that is open both to the difficulties they are currently facing as well as anything that might become possible.

Gunter had run his family's global business for many years and he was able to share a perspective that demonstrated this open, possibility mindset. 'I can't lead this business on my own' he said. 'I need great people to help me and my main job is to encourage their belief and potential.' Gunter listened and showed that he was open to his people's ideas. He went out of his way to show his colleagues that they were making valuable contributions to the company. And they then felt encouraged and motivated to do things differently and go that extra mile.

This possibility mindset clearly helped Gunter to build his relationships and generate an atmosphere of trust. It also helped his colleagues develop more of this mindset themselves. It was infectious.

Having such a positive attitude to growth and the development of potential is key to a possibility mindset. Instead of having an inner critic that is constantly driving us to be better than anyone else, the underpinning dialogue of a possibility mindset is more 'what could I get up to here?', 'how can I make a bigger difference?' and 'how can I help the people around me be more successful?'.

For people who want to lead, this mindset is potent. The focus on 'possibility' is underpinned by a focus on learning, improving and enjoying the journey.

What we also see with people who have this possibility mindset is their willingness to take on new challenges. They don't live life by always playing it safe. They enjoy being stretched and they embrace the unknown as part of their growth and development. This also makes them more resilient. People with this mindset expect setbacks and invite support. And they are open to feedback because that helps them to understand and grow. As a result they are quicker to rebound and try new approaches.

NOTICE NOW

- When have you been driven by fear?
- What's it like for you when you are driven by fear and what's it like to be around you when you are in this fearful mindset?
- When have you been inspired by possibility?
- How different is it for you when you are in this mindset and for others to be around you at such times?

Here is a poem which highlights the two mindsets. From the top read this poem and notice the fear. Then read it from the bottom up and notice the possibility.

Today everything went wrong
And I don't believe that
There's always a positive way to look at it.
If you consider those you care about,
They sometimes let you down.
Even if
People's intention may be different.
There is no greater good or higher purpose.
And it's not true that
It's in your attitude.
Because
Success can be achieved
Only when you are in control.
It's untrue that hope exists
And you surely agree that
Your world
Creates
Your thinking.
I didn't have a chance.
And you will never hear me say that
Today I made a difference

Inspired by Chanie Gorkin

Choose your mindset

I am not what happened to me, I am what I choose to become

Carl Jung

Your mindset is a choice and you can develop the ability to choose a possibility mindset everyday, if you want to. Neuroscience research tells us how plastic the brain is and how, through conscious practise, you can retrain your brain. But there will also be times when you fall back into old fearful patterns.

Around 10 years ago Ian was reading a book by Terry Pratchett to Immi, his daughter. In it, the main character is challenged to think in a way that changes her mindset and helps her to see the possibilities in her world. This started us thinking about a way of interrupting our own mindset and that of the leaders we work with. The following model helps us to choose our mindset and we think it accurately highlights the behaviours and responses we have observed in the world of leadership.

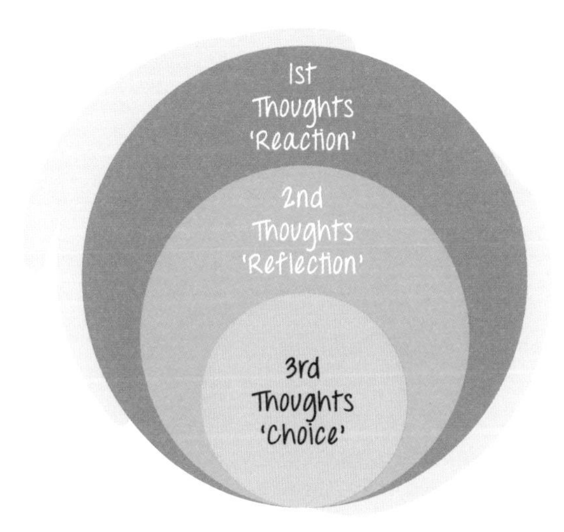

1st Thoughts – Reaction

We all spend time reacting to people and events and when we are in reaction it's more than likely that we will find ourselves being driven by fear. 1st Thought reaction is endemic and many people seem addicted to it. If you want to see great examples of 1st Thoughts in action, then trawl social media.

But if we can notice that we are 'in reaction' then we can start to see that it's a triggered response. If we can pause and remind ourselves that we have choice, then we can stop our knee-jerk response.

Notice your reactions

There are many ways to notice your reactive mindset. It may feel unbelievably fast and instinctive – a fight or flight response. You may find yourself tightening up physically. You might notice you get aggressive or start blaming others. Typically, your inner chatter will be focusing on either how stupid other people are or how dumb you have been!

And you will have distinct behavioural traits when you are in reaction. You might puff up or shrink back. You might become immediately confrontational or go away and complain to others. And when you are triggered in this way you probably think you are absolutely 100% right ... which of course makes other people 100% wrong.

2nd Thoughts – Reflection

The way we move beyond reaction is to reflect on what's going on. How come I'm having this reaction? Why am I feeling frustrated?' Why do I want to write that stinging response?

With 2nd Thought reflection we start to become curious and begin asking ourselves questions. What caused this reaction? What do my 1st Thoughts tell me about myself and my attitudes? Is there anything valuable about these 1st Thoughts? By reflecting on them we gain a wider perspective and a valuable opportunity to understand ourselves better.

Notice your reflections

Some people reflect by keeping a diary or journal. Others take time out on their own or go for a walk. Sometimes reflecting can be done with the help of another person who helps you to slow down and look at how you've been reacting.

A signal that you are in reflection is that you are calmer, you are focusing consciously on an issue and you are seeing that you have a choice. Like most things this becomes easier the more you practise and what we're often practising here, just to get to reflection, is letting go of being right.

3rd Thoughts – Choice

Sometimes, however, 2nd Thought thinking can feel like a handbrake. It might stop us reacting but it doesn't necessarily take us into possibility.

Our 3rd Thoughts connect us to our wiser self and allow us to make a choice. They may include everything we've learnt and everything we've understood about life. Our 3rd Thoughts are typically more inclusive, compassionate and authentic. If you think you are in 3rd Thoughts but still feeling negative, then you are simply still having 1st Thoughts which are masquerading as wisdom. 3rd Thoughts allow us to access the leadership mindset that takes us into possibility and clear response.

Notice your choice

When you are in this 'choice' mindset you will have a real sense of your own confidence. This may come through as genuine curiosity, openness or excitement. Typically, your inner voice will be interested both in what's happening now and in understanding the possibilities that are emerging.

Your behaviours will be different too. You might step into a conversation or ask for feedback and alternative ideas. You'll be happy to be challenged and if someone has a better idea than you then you will immediately consider it. Your focus will be on those around you, the bigger picture and moving things forward with energy.

CHOOSE NOW

Think of a real issue that is bothering you

- What are some of the 1st Thought reactions that catch you out?
- What do your 2nd Thought reflections tell you about these reactions?
- Using your 3rd Thoughts what choices become available to you from your possibility mindset?

Getting triggered

Just because you want to be in a possibility mindset does not mean, however, that you won't get triggered and have bad days. There will be situations, people and problems that will sometimes leave you feeling helpless, hopeless and worthless. If you have a tendency towards a fearful mindset then you may well beat yourself up at these times. Your inner dialogue will be telling you that once again you didn't get it right, once again you failed.

This is normal of course. You are back in reaction again – making up stories that confirm your worst view of yourself. This is where it's especially important to reflect. It's also a great time to ask for help! And more than anything we encourage you to cultivate self-compassion as a resource. None of us are perfect. None of us get it right all the time. As Leonard Cohen says: 'there is a crack in everything. That's how the light gets in.' And this is of course a brilliant 3rd Thought perspective.

Your leadership energies

You give life to what you bring your energy to

Another extraordinary resource available to us is our leadership energy. The subject of energies goes back to many of the ancient philosophies and they are still being used widely today. But let's bring some clarity to what we mean by energies, why we believe they are so important and how we can be creative with them.

Rachel is a director who is regularly described as a whirlwind by her colleagues. And you can probably imagine exactly how she shows up and what impact she has. She's fast, she has a big personality, she can be both hugely creative and sometimes more than a bit disruptive.

Rachel is a walking illustration of a leader who brings a particular brand of energy to her everyday activities and interactions. Such energy can be extremely useful and it also has its downsides. At its best it helps people open up new ways of working and thinking. At its worst it reduces focus and clarity and slows everything down.

The model opposite shows the four leadership energies and highlights some of the qualities we can associate with them.

As you read on we have explored in more detail what these energies can look like, how they can help your leadership and sometimes how they can get in the way.

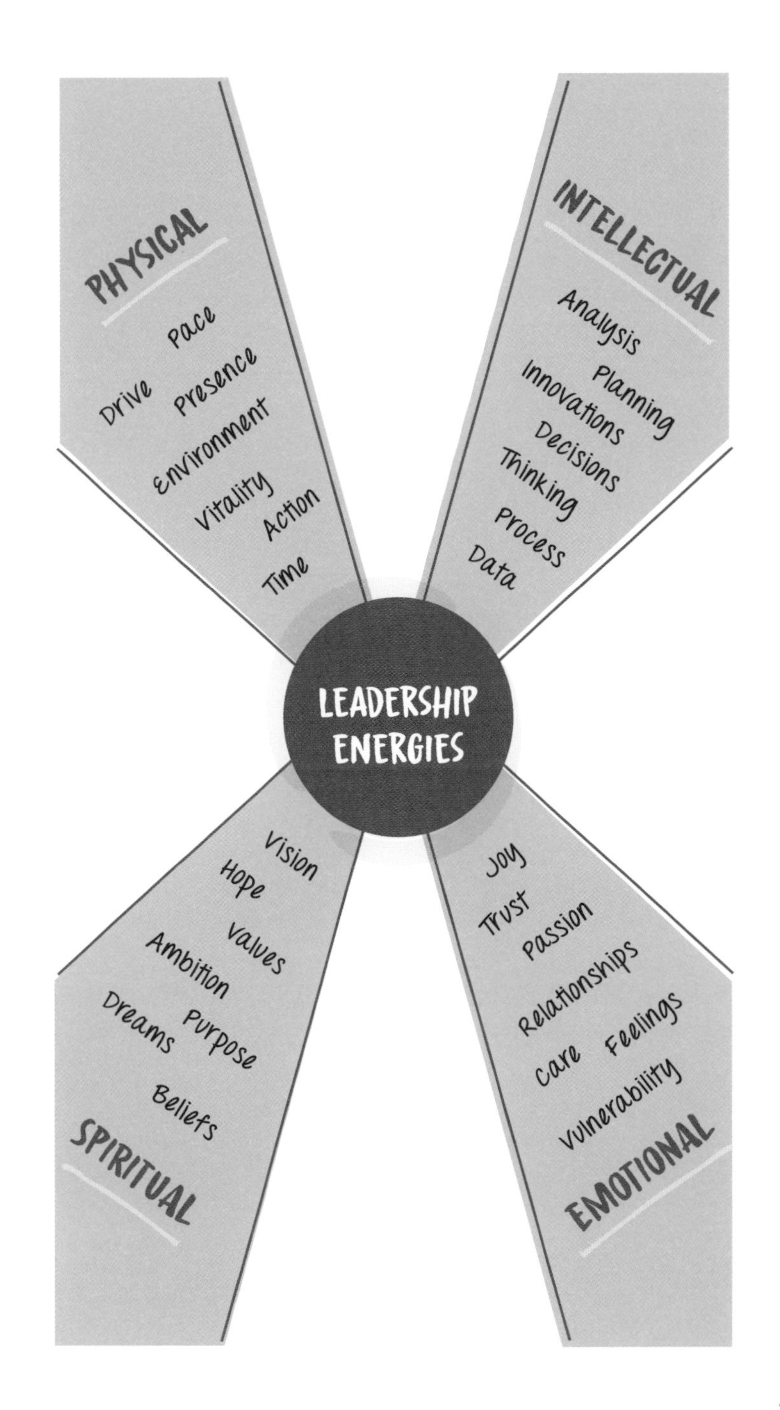
PHYSICAL
Pace
Drive
Presence
Environment
Vitality
Action
Time
INTELLECTUAL
Analysis
Planning
Innovations
Decisions
Thinking
Process
Data
LEADERSHIP ENERGIES
Vision
Hope
Values
Ambition
Purpose
Dreams
Beliefs
SPIRITUAL
Joy
Trust
Passion
Relationships
Care
Feelings
Vulnerability
EMOTIONAL

Physical: *body energy*

Physical energy is one that we need every day. It's the energy that gets us to work in the morning and which we use to drive our tasks and projects. Leaders who use this energy bring stamina and drive. It gives them presence and attack. It's also the energy that makes us feel alive.

- *The danger of too little physical energy:* If you have too little physical energy then others may feel as though you are exhausted or are going through the motions. You may even appear to be a passenger in the team. If you are leading a meeting and bring low physical energy then don't be surprised if people are listless or demotivated too.
- *The danger of too much physical energy:* When it's overplayed, this energy can leave other people feeling intimidated or even exhausted. It can also leave people feeling that they're not good enough when they can't run as far or as fast as you can.

Intellectual: *mind energy*

Intellectual energy helps us to be clear, focused and articulate. We join the dots, establish the strategy and we may even think out of the box. There is lots of this sort of energy in most working environments. Processes, agendas, strategies and plans are all indicative of intellectual energy.

- *The danger of too little intellectual energy:* When there is an absence of this energy things don't get thought through or we may tend to rely on 'gut' instinct. Sometimes this can compensate for clear thinking but it is a risky approach when important decisions need to be made.
- *The danger of too much intellectual energy:* But what happens when leaders are all over the detail all the time? The danger then

is that those around them may become risk-averse, thinking in straight lines and plodding through the days because there doesn't seem to be any room for creativity. When you bring too much intellectual energy it can leave other people feeling uninvolved and disengaged. Sometimes it even proves to be a hiding place for leaders who don't want to engage with people or problems.

Emotional: *heart energy*

Emotional energy is accessible when we are in touch with work that engages us and we feel passionate about. This is the energy of relationship, trust and joy. It's the energy of caring for others, wanting them to feel encouraged and being prepared to ask for support and challenge. It is also where our access to vulnerability lies and where we are most inviting. There can be a playful aspect to this energy but more than anything it will lead to people feeling that they belong and are valued.

- *The danger of too little emotional energy:* Have you ever worked in an organisation or team where relationships are small and transactional? Where there is little laughter or conversation? Too little emotional energy can create a grey and barren landscape and can lead to people not caring about their work or their team.
- *The danger of too much emotional energy:* Have you ever worked for a leader where feelings always dominate and evidence is ignored? Or where the desire of the leader to maintain harmony is the driving force? When a leader allows feelings to dominate in this way it can be very frustrating for others.

Spiritual: *belief energy*

When we are referring to spiritual energy we are not talking about faith or religion. Rather, this energy is all about belief and purpose. We are in touch with this energy when we know what's important to us and we act in accordance with our core values. It arises when we have vision and it is characterised by people living their dream.

Spiritual energy is underpinned by our belief. When you come across leaders who are inspired by belief you will find they often seem tireless. In essence what has happened is that their vision has become the source of their energy, they derive meaning from being connected to a greater cause and almost everything they do is seen in the context of that vision. Spiritual energy is at play when hope, ambition and purpose are alive. It's also present when we know 'why' the work we are doing matters.

- *The danger of too little spiritual energy:* When a leader doesn't bring enough spiritual energy then the teams they are leading can drift and uncertainty can prosper. People start to question what they are doing and what difference they are making. And there can be a real sense that 'nothing really matters'.
- *The danger of too much spiritual energy:* On the other side, when there is too much spiritual energy leaders can appear righteous or preachy. And when leaders are certain of their beliefs it can be very divisive. 'You are either with me or against me' is the paradigm here. In this sense people with too much spiritual energy can become very rigid. It can also become disheartening when belief trumps everything else and what you're aiming for seems unrealistic.

NOTICE NOW

- What do you notice about the energy of your own leadership, team and organisation?
- What's the dominant energy in your meetings?
- What energy, if you brought it, would make a difference?
- What have you lost sight of?

Using our energies creatively

The benefit of understanding and using these leadership energies is that they allow us to choose how we show up. They give us more options and opportunities in the way we interact with others.

For example, when we are imaginative with physical energy we may start to act in new ways and stretch further than we ever thought we could. When we are imaginative with our intellectual energy we might access innovation and discovery. With emotional energy we might dare to be different and with spiritual energy we might be open to the deepest change or inspiration.

By consciously choosing how to bring our energy to others we also create more possibility. We might choose to light up a conversation or pay attention to an important relationship and we might help people deepen their thinking. Choosing to use our energies in this way consciously helps our impact ... but it isn't always easy.

Robert is a leader who felt that the spark in his team was missing. His own dominant energy was intellectual and in his leadership he focused first on plans, structures and goals. He and his team were working hard but they weren't flowing.

When we introduced Robert to the idea of the energies he immediately saw what was going on. His organisation rewarded practical ideas and evidence-based solutions – i.e. intellectual energy – and his own leadership reflected this. It wasn't easy for him to change but he saw that what was needed was more passion, trust and purpose – in other words he needed to bring more emotional and spiritual energy, which would give people a feeling they were doing something worthwhile, together.

Robert's story is all too common. Most organisations that we work with overvalue physical energy, where they are being too busy, and intellectual energy, thinking that their plans will solve all their problems.

What they typically need is more emotional energy, where they are building trust and relationships, and spiritual energy, where they are finding a cause or mission that inspires them.

This doesn't mean that there isn't a place for intellectual and physical energy – clearly there is – but there needs to be much more focus on those aspects of leadership and culture that truly engage people.

So how can we be wholehearted and introduce new energy into our leadership? Robert's way was to explore his options using the energies as his lens. From then on he started to reduce the relentless focus on agendas and analysis and increase the focus on people's feelings, hopes and dreams. The team transformation was immediate and this missing conversation allowed more team spirit, collaboration and joy to appear.

CHOOSE NOW

- Think of a real situation where things aren't working as well as you would like.
- Notice which energies you use most and which energies are underused or missing.
- If you brought a different energy to this situation what difference would it make?
- Try it out. Bring this different energy in your own way as soon as possible and notice what impact it makes.

IN SUMMARY

This chapter was about:

- Starting to recognise when you are driven by fear or inspired by possibility
- Choosing your mindset
- Practising your leadership energies

Choosing between fear and possibility is a crucial practice for leaders. Combining this with an understanding of leadership energy will be extremely helpful as you continue to explore 4i Leadership. These perspectives are here at the beginning because they underpin much of what's to come and they help you to start a bolder conversation that matters. They are especially relevant when applied to all the ideas, stories and models that follow. So as you read on stay in a possibility mindset – much of what we've written is designed to encourage your 3rd Thought choices, and bring the energy that will stimulate your thinking.

Interrupt

In a room where people unanimously maintain a conspiracy of silence, one word of truth sounds like a pistol shot

Czesław Miłosz

the
'wake-up'
call
INTERRUPT
the
compelling
interrupt
you get
what you
tolerate

Interrupt

Interrupt is the first of the 4i's. We're talking here about positive interruption, that sudden insight that wakes us up and allows us to see a current situation in a completely new light. These interruptions are critical for two reasons – they highlight what's not working and they are a catalyst for new thinking and new action.

'You get what you tolerate' is a useful maxim to keep in mind when thinking about interruption. Where do you tolerate things that reduce possibilities or frustrate you? How do you interrupt what's going on in a way that is powerful, useful and leads to something better?

In this chapter we will explore the skill of leadership interruption, why it's so important and how to begin it. Interruption always has the potential to bring a different perspective and when done well creates the possibility for something new and powerful to emerge. The willingness to create positive interruption is one of the most important roles of a leader. In the following pages we will bring to life:

1. Why wake-up calls are essential
2. How to surface what we're tolerating
3. How to make compelling interruptions

The 'wake-up' call

Argue for your limitations and, sure enough, they're yours

Richard Bach

A few years ago Ian was working with a senior leader who found himself in a new role and a very challenging situation. The leader, Jim, had fallen into an unhelpful mindset and needed interrupting.

When he started in his new organisation Jim had brought with him a great sense of optimism and ambition and there was certainly an opportunity for him to make an impact. But after several months his perspective and attitude seemed to change. Instead of talking about what he wanted to achieve Jim began to speak more and more about the obstacles he was facing and what he had come to believe wasn't possible. His frustration was obvious; he couldn't see any way forward and he even began wondering why he ever thought he would be able to make a success of his career.

At moments like this interruption isn't only important; it's essential. But that doesn't make it easy. Ian waited for the right moment and, looking directly into Jim's eyes, said 'it sounds like they've got you'.

Jim is a no-nonsense leader and he came straight back at Ian. He argued his case vehemently, told Ian exactly what his problems were and the reasons why he hadn't made the progress he wanted. He was clearly cross with Ian's intervention and detailed all the organisational realities that justified his behaviour.

'Wow,' Ian said with a glint of humour when he'd run through his list, 'they've really got you'.

Jim had quite a reaction to this and looked like he was going to explode. Then something shifted. And with a huge release of breath

Jim said 'Damn it! You're right. They really got me', and they both laughed long and loud.

After this wake-up call Jim and Ian talked about the weight of culture and how easy it is to lose perspective. As well as his own needs Jim was facing other people's doubts and lack of enthusiasm. He recognised that he had lost energy and had started to tolerate other people's poor behaviour and attitudes.

Jim's case isn't unusual. Leaders at all levels often find themselves arguing long and hard for their limitations and why the change they want simply won't or can't occur. It's true to say that in some instances the change might not be worth it – you don't have to interrupt everything – but when you really need or want change then you have to interrupt the story!

In Jim's case what had happened was that he'd allowed himself to become a much smaller leader than he wanted to be. His need to fit in, to be accepted by his peers and to be seen as reasonable had compromised his ability to be bold and make big decisions. Helping Jim to confront his story in such a provocative way had allowed him to see how he was limiting himself and enabled him to get back in touch with what he really cared about. He wanted to make a difference and he was prepared to be relentless about improving performance. If that meant a few people getting upset then he was more than ready for that to lead to a bolder conversation.

This interruption gave Jim his mojo back and, more importantly, helped him get back in touch with the leadership he wanted to bring – and which the organisation desperately needed.

NOTICE NOW

- Where are you arguing for your own limitations?
- Who aren't you listening to?
- Where are you asleep at the wheel?

You get what you tolerate

Don't ask why something's not working, ask why you're participating in it

---

Tolerance is a wonderful human quality, it allows us to be compassionate and gives our overly critical minds a break. Where it becomes unhelpful is when we start to tolerate behaviours or norms that drain our energy and hold us back. Our lives and the organisations we work in are full of this type of unhelpful tolerance. Here are just a few of the things we've found people tolerating over the years:

short termism poor behaviours
the limiting stories we tell ourselves
lack of creativity no real vision
unethical practice ineffective processes inequality
mediocrity unhealthy work/life balance
draining relationships

Interruption is powerful when you see and address issues like these and it is a critical skill for leaders. It's a potent conversation that allows you and those around you to 'wake up' to what you've stopped noticing and see where it is having a negative impact.

NOTICE NOW

- What are you tolerating in your world today?
- What are the benefits and consequences of tolerating it?

With this in mind let's look now at one of the essential insights about interruption. It isn't always about what's not working. It may be what we tell ourselves about what's not working! In other words it's often our thinking that limits us, not the reality. In this respect we need to look both at the facts and also the stories that surround the challenges we are facing.

Facts and stories

My life has been full of terrible misfortunes, most of which never happened – Michel de Montaigne

FACTS AND STORIES

WHAT ARE YOU TOLERATING?

WHAT ARE THE FACTS?

Provable
Evidence-based

WHAT ARE THE UNHELPFUL STORIES?

From our fearful mindset

NEW PERSPECTIVE

Applying the facts to the stories

When looking at our life and work let's be clear – there are loads of things that frustrate us and things that don't occur in the way we expect. It also seems to be a human trait to make up stories that are unhelpful, which sustain the status quo or even make difficult situations worse.

A few years ago we had a conversation with Jason, a team leader who had asked for some coaching. He had a number of things that he was dissatisfied and frustrated about. There was a whole set of events happening at work that had led him to think about moving on. His performance was under scrutiny by his boss. His career wasn't progressing as he was hoping and he was struggling in his relationship at home with his wife. And as he started to talk about these aspects of his life it became clear that something needed to be interrupted. It was also clear that there was a huge gap between the facts surrounding his circumstances and the stories he was telling himself about them.

Jason's work performance

The story – The story Jason was telling himself about work was that he was out of his depth. Everyone else appeared able to tough it out so his stress must be a personal failing. He had begun to believe that perhaps he'd be better off elsewhere and that he should find a more sedate role.

The facts – Jason was in one of the most challenging and competitive areas of his organisation. He was a high performer but the current culture was tough. Targets were high and the pacesetting environment drove everyone to extremes.

Jason's career

The story – The story Jason had started to believe was that he wasn't a good enough leader and his potential didn't match that of his colleagues. He believed others were acutely aware of his failings and that he'd been found out. He was telling himself that the level he had reached was the level he would always be at, and although this was disheartening it was probably deserved.

The facts – Jason was a very successful business leader and had narrowly missed a recent promotion. He had received excellent feedback and was respected by his peers. A career move hadn't come this time but nobody doubted it was well within his reach.

Jason's home life

The story – The story Jason had started to believe was that he was failing both as a husband and a father and he was worried that the magic had gone from his marriage. As a result he'd started to wonder whether his efforts had been worth it, whether his wife cared about him and whether they'd stay together.

The facts – Jason had been married for eight years to his childhood sweetheart and had two lovely children who he was proud of. They had a home they loved, which they had renovated imaginatively. However, this project combined with being parents had made it a challenging few years. He and his wife were often exhausted.

Are Jim and Jason's circumstances and stories exceptional? Not in our experience. We meet clients every week who tell us stories of a similar nature. And we find that it can be helpful for people facing such challenges to separate the facts from the stories they are telling themselves.

Facts are all to do with exploring what is actually going on or understanding what has truly happened. In contrast, stories are the interpretation we give to the situations we face – and these may not be true at all! Indeed, we make up stories all the time and when we are in a fearful mindset these stories may overwhelm us and cause us to lose sight of the facts.

The idea of looking at facts vs stories was created in a workshop that we were running a few years ago. The team we were working with had been through a tough year and their version of their current reality was very negative. In fact they'd had considerable success. Interrupting their thinking in this way helped them to get things into perspective.

NOTICE NOW

Think of a situation that you haven't been able to resolve either at work or home.

- What's the worst story you tell yourself about this situation?
- What are the facts?

If you find it difficult to sort out the facts from the story then this is a great time to ask for help. Simply ask someone you trust to help you highlight any stories you are telling yourself and the real facts of this situation.

Now with this in mind let's look at how we can interrupt unhelpful stories and disempowering realities.

The compelling interrupt

"Make it dark, make it grim, make it tough, but then, for the love of God, tell a joke."

Joss Whedon

Interruption, when sourced from possibility, is a crucial and powerful skill for leaders. It's interruption that brings about change and in turn creates space for new choices.

Here are four ways of bringing interruption to what you're tolerating. Each one has its own flavour and impact. As we bring them to life you'll notice that they tend to ramp up in their intensity. Keep in mind those issues or behaviours that you have been tolerating and, as you read on, notice what effect these interruptions might have.

Bring curiosity

Curiosity can get you into, or out of, trouble. Use it well

Your curiosity as a leader is a powerful tool for engendering change and it is especially useful when you notice that the story you and others are telling is at odds with the facts.

Curiosity comes to life when you start asking questions that help find new perspectives. So, for example, what is the story that is being told? Is it a useful story? What evidence do you have that it is true?

In simple terms, at this level of interruption you are encouraging a change in script and looking for a more empowering story that will, in turn, drive a different behaviour. So instead of feeling helpless in the face of frustration you recognise that there is much you can do with a different mindset. In other words, you are trying to connect to a sense of what's possible.

To bring this to life let's take Liz, who was curious about a key member of her team, George, who she felt was underperforming. She started the interruption by inviting him to a one-to-one conversation and sharing her perspectives with him.

'I know you have enormous knowledge and experience' Liz told George 'and yet it's been bothering me that you don't seem to be enjoying your work. I've been wondering whether this is true and whether you believe you have the opportunities to express yourself in this team. I'm also curious about the George I know who has so much humour and creativity out of work. I wonder what impact you might have if you expressed that part of yourself more?'

In this example Liz is inviting George to think bigger and feel a sense of possibility that he might not have felt before. Liz isn't telling George to be different. She's inviting him to wake up to his potential and change the way he's thinking and contributing to the team.

With this interruption George started to break out of his limited thinking about what he could do. He started to contribute more and bring his experience and creativity to the team.

This type of curiosity is a great awakener and is a potent way of helping people, teams and organisations look at things from a different perspective. The best leaders we've worked with are always curious.

Interrupt from the future

The future is always calling – are you listening?

There are times in our lives when we know what really matters to us, when we are being called by a compelling vision. At these times our belief is strong and the story that 'this is worth it' or that 'I'm going to make a difference' is fuel for our ambition.

At other times, however, especially when we listen to an inner voice that is fearful in nature, we can lose sight of all that is dear to us. It's at times like this that interrupting from the future is a powerful way to help us realign.

It's with this in mind that we often ask our clients to clarify their sense of purpose, their dream and their heart's desire. Are they in touch and making progress toward their future or have they begun to accept things as they are?

Interruptions from the future are hugely helpful in reminding us that we have a deeper purpose. So how do you interrupt from the future?

It can help to challenge yourself here. What are you like when you are '100% all-in'? What would happen if you gave up on your dream? What one action could you take today that would be a first step to the future you want?

In a recent piece of work we undertook with Megan she was feeling close to despair about her organisation and her part in it. More than this, she didn't know what she could do about it. But when we asked her whether she could be a 'leader for hope' she seemed to come to life. 'But how would I do that?' she asked. 'Well ... all it would mean is that in every conversation, relationship and project you would put hope into the agenda. It could be planting a seed of hope or making a big bold statement about hope. It could be about being more optimistic yourself or inviting positivity from others.' And with this range of options Megan was back in touch with something that felt possible for her and in an instant she was re-energised.

This was an interruption on a personal level but you can of course interrupt from the future on a grander scale as well. This is exemplified when you have a dream of something bigger and better that encourages and inspires others. We explore how imagination can fuel dreams, causes and possibilities in the next chapter.

Speak your truth

Find your truth and your voice will follow

Speaking truth to power is an interruption that takes both commitment and integrity. It is about courageous speaking. The risk here is that the other person may feel overly challenged and at its worst you may fall into argument. At your best, however, you bring all of yourself to the relationship and create the possibility for a breakthrough.

Hasan is the CEO of a multinational company and a major influence within his industry. Yet when we started working with his senior team it all felt very flat. His team were polite but there was absolutely no spark, and the distraction in the room indicated a distinct lack of engagement. So we asked Hasan for a straight conversation and shared our experience. Hasan looked slightly abashed. His people had done something similar before, he explained. It wasn't new for them. Perhaps we needed to do something different.

This might have been true but we also knew that Hasan had spent all day checking his phone and participating sporadically. We spoke this truth to him too and suddenly we had his full attention. 'You see a team is always a response to a leader', we told him, 'and if you want us to do brilliant work with your team then you, the CEO, have to be brilliant too. If you want your people to be more open, more engaged and more visionary then you need to bring those qualities yourself –

not expect us to do all the work for you'.

This was one of those moments when we thought we might get fired. Hasan clearly hadn't been expecting this sort of challenge and he wasn't used to it. But after some deep breaths he nodded and asked us what we wanted him to do.

We invited Hasan to share his vision in a way he had never done before. We asked him to share deeply where he had come from, why the company was important to him, what he believed about people and what he wanted to achieve in the world. We also asked him to talk about how important his team were to him in supporting his aims and ambitions and to ask, powerfully and vulnerably, for their help.

In that moment it was in the balance. We weren't at all sure what we were going to get from Hasan but when the time came this reserved man stood up and spoke to his team, senior engineers all, about where he had come from, the deep struggles he had overcome in his life and why, as a result, the company was so important to him. He gave his people a clear understanding of the purpose and mission that drove him and what he thought that, together, they could achieve. This wasn't about the business. This was about a greater cause. And his team not only applauded, a number of them were deeply moved. And in that moment, in the telling of that story, the breakthrough arrived.

In our work we are privileged enough to see and hear all sorts of courageous acts of leadership. Hasan's was one of the most powerful. It interrupted the existing reality. It shocked the system. It opened people's eyes to the potential they might achieve.

Draw your line in the sand

Sometimes there is nothing left but your integrity

This is the interruption you go to when you've tried everything and the only way forward you can see is to draw your line in the sand. This requires you to stand for what you truly believe in and it can, and often does, mean creating discomfort. This is when you are holding the tension in a scenario where, for you, there is no further compromise to make.

For many of us, this can be the hardest interruption to make without putting others in a corner. It's when our 'fearful mindset' frequently kicks in and shouts at us to run or attack – neither of which is helpful.

Andrew, who headed up the health and safety function for a major UK company, was in a very hard situation. His company, in striving for new business, was pushing its sales team to take unacceptable risks. The need to meet deadlines and drive for profit had already led to a string of car accidents directly attributable to this initiative. And next time, Andrew feared this pressure could easily lead to a death. But whenever he spoke about his concerns, nobody was listening. He was consistently being ignored by his boardroom colleagues.

When we asked how important the issue was for him, Andrew replied immediately that it was career defining. If his boss wouldn't listen to him and back him then he would resign, he said. And it was at this moment that Andrew broke free. He was no longer constrained by the normal rules of behaviour that governed his working life – this was his line in the sand.

So Andrew didn't wait. He gave up playing safe. That evening he went around to the home of his boss and knocked at the door. He didn't announce his arrival, he just turned up. And when his boss saw him on the doorstep he immediately said 'This must be important. Come in.' As a result of this interruption Andrew and his boss had their first serious conversation about safe working practices, which ultimately led to an immediate change in policy.

Such active interruption is dramatic and it may not always be appreciated. However, sometimes it is the only way of truly getting someone's attention. And when the issue is so important and you've tried everything else then it can be exactly the right thing to do.

Your line in the sand: three principles

Drawing your line in the sand takes courage and can have extreme consequences. It's important to be clear about any interruption you are going to make and for this one you will need to be especially clear on what you stand for. Here are three principles to keep in mind.

1. Clarify your intent. Why are you making this dramatic interruption? What are the consequences if you don't? Be sure that it is important enough to you to take a 'no compromise' stand.
2. Make the interruption in a way that builds your relationships. Bring your interruption in support of others and their success. Be as invitational as possible.
3. Bring conviction and courage. Drawing a line in the sand can often feel scary. People often don't enjoy being challenged and you may not be popular when you bring your unambiguous perspective. So again, make sure it matters enough to you and have your own support in place.

Notice that all of these interruptions are designed to create possibility, not diminish it. So take a moment to consider where you need to make a compelling interruption.

NOTICE NOW

- Where would curiosity be helpful today?
- Where do you need to bring more possibility thinking?
- Where do you need to speak more courageously?
- Are you clear on your line in the sand?

Don't dilute your impact

Never touch anything with half of your heart

Even when we are clear that there are things that need to be interrupted it's not always easy to do. Here are the three most common ways we dilute or choose to avoid an interruption.

1. The half-hearted interrupt

This is when you know something isn't working but you don't bring enough conviction to your interruption. For example, you start speaking and then pull back – or you set up an important conversation and then don't bring enough clarity or commitment to what you are saying.

People will immediately know if you are committed or not. Take Mike, who wanted to raise important issues in the project he was part of. He always started with good intentions but was worried about overstepping the mark and causing friction. Every time people pushed back on his views his fearful mindset would kick in and he would either back down or speak in a way that diluted his impact. So, in the face of Mike's half-hearted interruption, the status quo was maintained.

2. The righteous interrupt

Another term for this sort of interrupt is 'I know best' or 'look how wrong you are' – and if you bring this attitude you are doomed to fail. The problem is not so much whether you are right or wrong in your interruption, it's the rigidity that you bring with it. When you are righteous it's disengaging and tends to make people feel defensive. Your intention may be to get people to pay attention to something that isn't working but if you are attached to being right then you can guarantee that people will resist or resent your ideas, however valuable they might be.

3. Wilful blindness

Sometimes it might just feel too uncomfortable to interrupt, even when you know that what is occurring is clearly unproductive or damaging. At these times you may be tempted to ignore what's in front of you. When you do this you focus instead on what's easy to tackle and avoid the big stuff. Who of us, for example, hasn't avoided a conversation because it just feels too difficult or too inflammatory? At such times we always have many excuses that justify our behaviour and none of them solve the problem. The danger of wilful blindness is that you can end up colluding with the very thing that you believe needs interrupting.

We all sometimes manage to dilute our impact. In some ways it's part of our desire to fit in, not upset others and not find ourselves outside whichever group, team or organisation we're part of. It's usually our fearful mindset that encourages us to do this.

IN SUMMARY

This chapter was about:

- Waking up to possibility
- Identifying what you are tolerating
- The skill of making a compelling interruption

This is just the beginning. In the next chapter we are heading into imagination where we will consider what you stand for, how you want to be as a leader and how to create something much better than what you are currently tolerating.

Imagine

What are you going to do with your one wild and precious life?

Mary Oliver

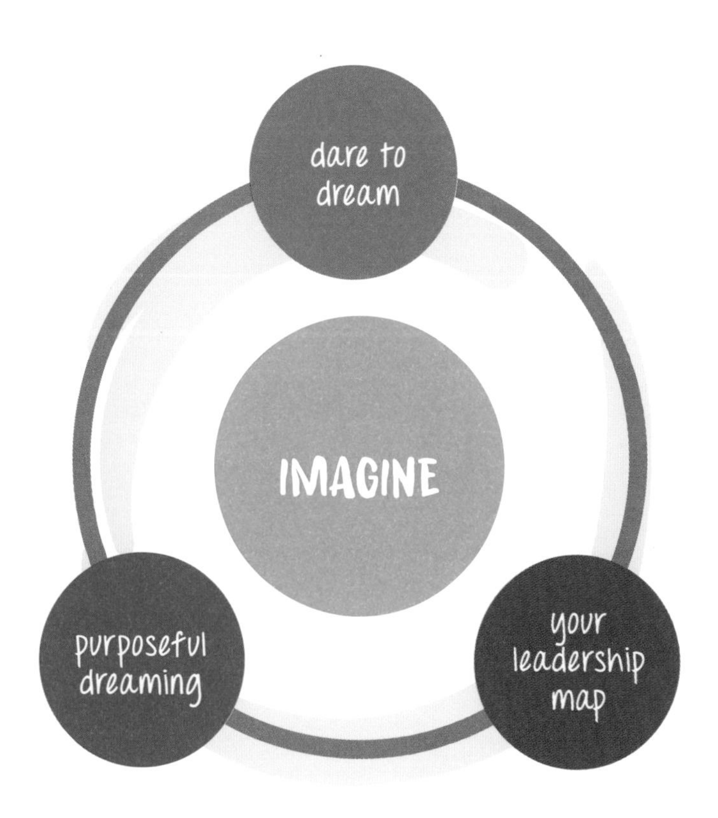
dare to
dream
IMAGINE
purposeful
dreaming
your
leadership
map

Imagine

Imagine is the second of the 4i's. This is the ability to stretch our thinking so that it's exciting and purposeful. It's about daring to go beyond what currently exists. It's about your dream.

You've thought about interruption and have identified some issues that you are no longer prepared to tolerate. How can you imagine a future that is different, better, brilliant? Imagine having such a powerful dream that it fuels your ambition and energises others to join up with you.

Do you have such a dream already? This chapter will help you create an inspiring platform for your own leadership and will cover:

1. Daring to dream
2. Creating your leadership map
3. Bringing purpose to your dream

Dare to dream

Anything or anyone that does not bring you alive is too small for you

David Whyte

Is it too much of a stretch to expect work and our lives to be inspiring? Not at all. Indeed, those leaders who want to make a big impact in the world know how essential it is to have a vision that engages and ignites others.

We need people who can dream powerfully – people who push the boundaries of possibility and challenge the existing reality with their imagination. That's when breakthroughs occur. And it's these breakthroughs that make us fit for the future.

Let's consider Mo Ibrahim, a leader with extraordinary vision, who Anthony had a conversation with several years ago.

After a stellar career in O2, Mo Ibrahim developed a very successful mobile phone consultancy. This enterprise made him a multimillionaire but it wasn't until he sold that business that Mo put himself behind his real dream. And that dream is to end poverty in Africa.

Clearly Mo Ibrahim is a man who has a powerful cause. He makes us want to cheer! However, what we can also see from his story are two key aspects of having a big dream.

First, it doesn't matter if your dream is completely unrealistic. Do we think Mo Ibrahim will ever end poverty in Africa? No. But will working to make his dream a reality have an impact and make a difference? Absolutely. What is clear is that you need a big dream to tackle big issues and in Mo's case this is a cause absolutely worth serving.

Second, it is evident that Mo Ibrahim's dream is completely aligned with who he is as a human being. His values are all about justice, fairness and innovation. His belief about Africans is that they are 'heroic entrepreneurs'. He is a man who is full of imagination.

Furthermore, he isn't just dreaming about the future, he's doing something about it. If you want to make your dream a reality then you will need to bring your full commitment.

Mo Ibrahim showed exactly such a level of purpose. His drive and determination has made a difference to the everyday lives of thousands of people across Africa. His purpose shows up in the £100m foundation he has set up to encourage others who share his ambition. And his £5m annual prize for the most ethical leader in Africa demonstrates the highest level of commitment to deliver change.

Your dream may focus on a local or a global issue but, whatever the scale, be in no doubt you will need to bring imagination and purpose if you want it to flourish and grow.

We can be clear about our dream but that doesn't mean it's easy to bring to life. In the example above, Mo had to gather his courage and commit to the cause that he cared about.

When you are dreaming big you will need to harness your qualities and beliefs too. These could include:

This focus on imagining doesn't feature much in MBA courses and it's easy to be cynical about it all. The Return On Investment of dreams is, after all, pretty low. How will a dream help you meet this year's targets?

And yet it's the dream that is exciting, that stirs us and gives us and others a sense of meaning and purpose. It's in our imagining that we start to see the possibilities for development, innovation and change. Just think of Martin Luther King and his 'I have a dream' speech. If he had stood up that day and shared his critical path analysis to racial equality it would surely not have been that seminal moment that inspired millions.

NOTICE NOW

- **Where can you see the need for a dream?**
- **What difference would having a bigger dream make?**

Leadership is always personal

People follow you before they follow your dream

At the heart of your leadership is this – people want to know what you are all about. They might understand what your role is, but what they really want to hear about is what matters to you and the personal values that guide you. In other words, they want to know whether you are a leader they can trust and believe in.

To help with this question let's talk about Richard, a very thoughtful leader who had agreed to speak to a new intake of graduates. Perhaps rashly, the graduates had been advised that they could ask Richard anything they liked about leadership and so, after he had said a few words about the business, we came to the Q&A session. True to form the first question, asked with a certain bravado, was: 'Hi Richard, can you tell us about a time where you really messed up?'

Richard took some time before answering but eventually he looked up and replied. 'The biggest mistake I ever made was to put work before my marriage and as a result of that I lost the woman I loved. You see, work can be exciting and adrenaline-fuelled but it isn't everything. You need to work out for yourselves what's most important and however well your career is going you need to remember to pay fierce attention to the things that matter most to you.'

Richard had answered honestly and with far more vulnerability than the graduates had expected. He said he wished that at their age someone had given him the opportunity to explore what he truly stood for. It would have made all the difference. So in his anecdote he told his audience exactly what he was all about and how that helped him stand for what really mattered. He went on to talk about how this had helped him form his guiding principles for leadership. And when we asked these young graduates how they felt about his story it was clear that they had all been deeply touched and inspired. They had just met a leader who, for them, had fully shown up and who was able to deeply connect his leadership with his personal values and beliefs.

Over the next few pages we're going to help you define what you stand for and what matters to you. We call this your Leadership Map. This map will help you identify what it is about you 'as a leader' that would have anybody want to follow you. It will also help you clarify your dream and the journey you want to take people on.

Your leadership map

Start with wild hope and irrational desire

Daring to dream is enlivening but how does leadership support your dream?

Around 15 years ago we were working with a graduate intake in a multinational organisation on their leadership. The work was inspiring, but we hadn't yet found a simple and effective model that the students could take away and apply. We took a step back between workshops and thought about what would make a difference here.

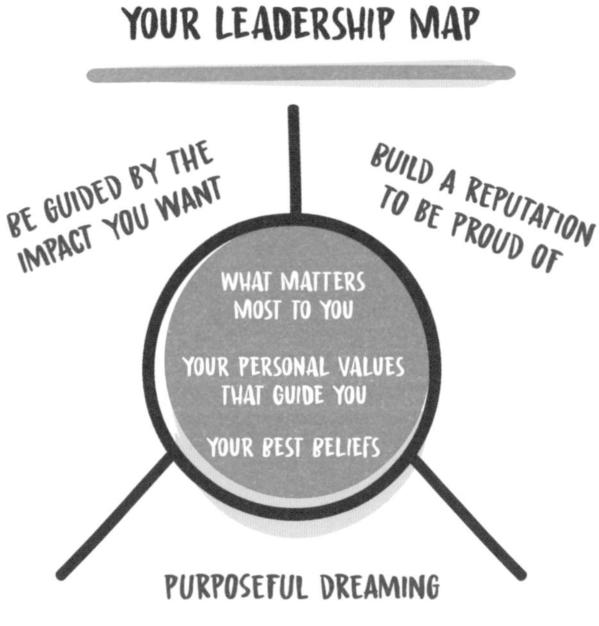

YOUR LEADERSHIP MAP

BE GUIDED BY THE IMPACT YOU WANT

BUILD A REPUTATION TO BE PROUD OF

WHAT MATTERS MOST TO YOU

YOUR PERSONAL VALUES THAT GUIDE YOU

YOUR BEST BELIEFS

PURPOSEFUL DREAMING

What emerged was the Leadership Map. It transformed everything. For the students it provided a personal compass that would guide them throughout their careers. For us it created a model that has formed an essential underpinning for all the consulting we have done with over 10,000 leaders across the world. So, this is your opportunity to do something that will have an immediate impact on your leadership. Over the following pages we are going to explore this with you and to get the most out of this it will be helpful to find some free space and genuine curiosity.

Take some time with this section and, before you start, be aware that there are a few things to keep in mind.

Few of the leaders we have worked with in this territory are used to being asked to apply their imagination in quite this way. Almost all of them find it an affirming and energising experience. Here it is not helpful to look for targets, business goals or strategies. Rather, when we exercise our imagination it starts in our heart and soul, with wild hope and irrational desire.

And don't start analysing your dream; that's a sure way to restrict yourself and it will simply frustrate you. Remember the concept of energies and especially bear in mind your spiritual and emotional energy. Consciously choose to bring both in order to clarify and get in touch with what you want. Be ready to bring your passion, your openness and your vulnerability.

Also watch out for easy or quick answers. Indeed, it can be helpful to take this exercise and these questions with you on a long walk. Or take some time one evening in front of a fire. Or sit by the sea or a river and ponder. There's no right way to get to your answers and we do know that finding the right environment can be important.

So, look for the spark that excites and inspires you and let's get started.

What matters most to you?

Knowing what matters is the bedrock of personal leadership

At the core of your map lies this question – what matters most to you? This is a key question for leaders because these things guide us in our dreams and our choices whether we're conscious of them or not.

What's most important to us shapes everything we do and underpins our sense of purpose. So for example, a leader like Mo Ibrahim, for whom poverty in Africa matters hugely, used this as a powerful motivation to guide his choices, conversations and dreams.

It's also important for the people you lead to know what really matters to you because it helps them connect to you and gives them confidence. Some of the things that matter most to us include:

making a difference
family & friends the environment
ending poverty success
helping others doing a great job
creating opportunities

These are just a few of our examples and we're sure you will have your own list. So start clarifying for yourself what matters most to you and what causes you believe in. If you have multiple answers then focus on those that give you the greatest uplift in energy. If it helps, you can also think about where you are most passionate or what makes your heart sing.

Once you are clear about what matters most to you then see if you can identify what's shaped your life in this way. For example, an experience with unfairness may shape our view on justice and equality. Or an experience with generosity and kindness may shape our views on how best to treat those around us.

Understanding where your passion comes from and being able to articulate it to others is extremely powerful. This is why leadership is personal; Richard's story was so engaging because he linked what mattered most to him to the leadership challenges he encountered.

NOTICE NOW

- What matters most to you?
- Why does it matter so much?
- What difference would it make if you were more focused on it?

What are your personal values?

Values are like fingerprints. Nobody's are the same but you leave them all over everything you do – Elvis

We also put personal values at the centre of the leadership map. We describe these as those deep-seated principles that underpin life, provide us with a moral compass and give us a clear sense of the right thing to do. If you haven't looked at your personal values for a while then this is a good opportunity to reconnect with them and clarify what you really stand for. It's critical for leaders to know and let other people know what values they live by. So take a moment and think deeply about which two or three values describe you best. These will be values that resonate with you and remind you of what you are all about.

Over the years this has been a cornerstone for us both. The key for us was to choose the values that represent who we are when we feel genuinely strong in ourselves.

Once we knew what they were we then had to bring them to life by noting down what they meant for us. For Anthony, loyalty is all about his commitment to other people and seeing things through. And for Ian, integrity is all about honesty, truthfulness and standing for what he believes in. It's this ability to describe our values, what they mean to us and why they matter, that makes them powerful.

NOTICE NOW

- What three values do you stand for above all else?
- What do these values mean to you?
- What in your life has shaped these values?

What are your best beliefs?

A funny thing happens when you start to believe in yourself. Other people start to believe in you too – Anon

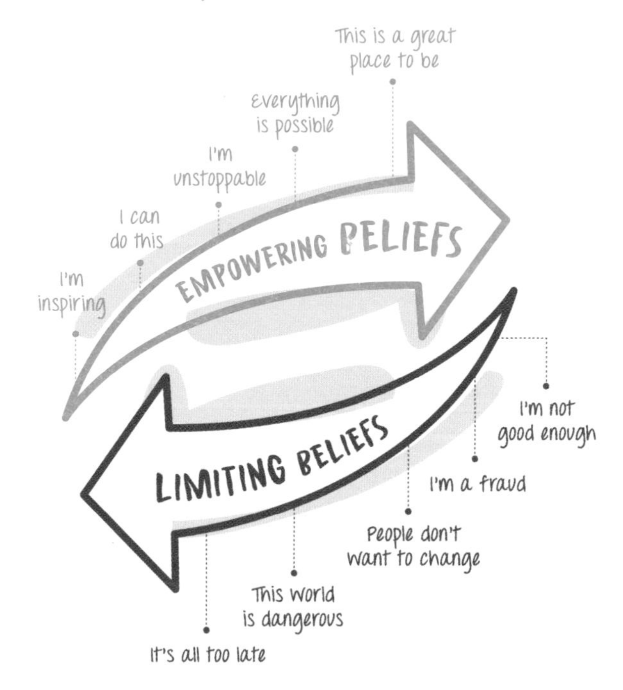

Our personal beliefs run in parallel to our personal values and they also underpin our leadership. Our beliefs affect our mindset and we can choose to believe things that empower us or limit us.

There are hundreds of beliefs that you can choose to live by. Remember that your beliefs aren't necessarily true but they are powerful – so it's important to choose the ones that are useful rather than ones that hold you back. The model opposite identifies some of the empowering and limiting beliefs that people often hold.

What we are asking here is for you to look for beliefs that represent you at your best and be aware of the beliefs that limit you. And with this in mind consider what difference having such beliefs might make on people and the world around you.

For example, think for a moment about adopting the belief '*I'm inspiring*' and consider what behaviours such a belief drives and what impact it might have. It might help you to bring more positivity and vision. It might remind you of how you engage other people. It might help reconnect you with a deeper sense of purpose.

A key reminder here is to remember when this has been real for you. There will have been times when you were inspiring, when you were in the zone, when you felt on top of the world! And at such times you were probably at your most engaging and fun to be around.

In contrast, succumbing to a belief such as '*I'm not good enough*' can lead you to avoid taking on new challenges or getting involved when you could really make a difference. Our limiting beliefs tend to drive us toward fear whereas our empowering beliefs take us toward possibility.

So choose those beliefs you want, build your relationship with them and let them underpin your confidence and fuel your behaviour and impact.

CHOOSE NOW

Limiting beliefs

- What are the unhelpful limiting beliefs that you choose to hold about yourself? Just listen to that negative voice in your head that's driven by your fearful mindset.
- How are these limiting beliefs getting in the way and holding you back?
- Can you provide any evidence that choosing to believe the worst about yourself helps you in any way at all?

Empowering beliefs

- Think of a time when you were at your best and when you felt most connected to what is important to you – a time that you are proud to say represents the very best of your values and your behaviours.
- What positive belief did you hold about yourself at that point?
- If you choose to act from this belief today what starts to become possible?

Be guided by the impact you want

Your impact shapes the way other people show up

Impact is all about how we want other people to feel and the possibilities it creates. Take the example of Sam who inherited a team that wasn't performing to its full potential. Guided by her values and beliefs Sam was clear about the impact she wanted to make. She wanted her people to be stimulated by the work, find the joy that can be experienced in a high performing team and use that to deliver brilliant results. To do that she helped people to understand what their individual success would look like and how they could help one another. Within a few months there was a significant change in culture and Sam was leading one of the highest trust teams in her organisation.

When we know the impact we want to have then it's essential we are guided by that intent. For example, what is the impact you want to have on others that will help them feel valued, confident or enlivened? Or what will stimulate the creativity of your colleagues, your team or those closest to you?

Once you know what impact you want to have you can then consider what actions, behaviours or characteristics you need to bring that would help you have that impact.

This isn't necessarily easy. It might be a stretch. But remember you are already making an impact whether you like it or not. Leaders understand this and they focus on showing up in a way that helps them make a positive impact on the people they want to lead.

NOTICE NOW

- What impact do you most (and least) want to have on others?
- If you were guided more often by the impact you want, how would that affect your leadership?

Build a reputation to be proud of

The truth about reputation is that whether you want it or not, you've already got one.

A reputation is a story, and can be influenced by your impact. It can also be a calling from the leader you want to become.

In a workshop a few years ago Freddie was asked to think about the reputation she would most want and following some reflection she came back into the room ashen-faced. We asked her how she had got on and she said 'I am 53 years old and for the first time in my career I realise I want to be known as someone inspiring' 'So why the long face?' we enquired and she replied, 'Because I have absolutely no idea how to achieve this'.

This breakthrough led to a great conversation for Freddie and she started to use her insight to explore how she could bring more inspiration to her life. This wasn't an easy thing for her to take on but it became a guiding principle for her leadership.

It's interesting that when we ask people to get personal and think about their reputation they often find it awkward. Perhaps this is because they confuse a desired reputation with arrogance. But a desired reputation is simply a lever to motivate ourselves. If we want other people to say we are empowering, for example, then we can start to work out how to behave in an empowering fashion.

Of course, if you don't care what others say about you, that's fine but beware – it can become a problem when your reputation gets in the way of what matters most to you. So, for example, if you want to be known as someone who gets the best out of people but you have a reputation for being ruthless then that might stop some people wanting to work with you.

NOTICE NOW

- What is the best thing anyone could say about you?
- What do you already have to be proud of?

Purposeful dreaming

The two most important days in your life are the day you are born and the day you find out why

Mark Twain

So you've explored why anyone would want to be led by you. The next question is what journey are you taking people on? This is where purposeful dreaming is so vital.

There are two aspects to purposeful dreaming – the dream and cause that inspires you and the purpose and commitment that will bring that dream to life. Remember here that dreams show us a glimpse of a possible future – that's what makes them exciting. But they aren't safe. They can upset the existing order and lead to a radical shift in trajectory. For example some dreams might substantially affect your life and those around you.

So, what is your dream and what makes it worth going for?

Start by exploring the following questions:

- What have you always dreamt of doing?
- What would feel exciting and creative to you?
- What would give you a greater sense of purpose or meaning?
- What is compelling for you?
- What cause is worth serving?
- What's the difference you want to make in the world?

Dare to write down words that capture your dream. Look for the spark and sense of excitement that lights you up. And if you're ready, or it's helpful, invite someone you trust to prompt your imagination with further questions and enquiries. Choose to do this from your empowering belief, it will embolden you.

Rarely does your dream arrive fully formed but it can be helpful to start describing what it could look and feel like in the future. Once you have started to dream you can then imagine where it will lead. Keep in mind the following questions which will help clarify what this future could look like.

Now consider how to bring that dream alive with commitment and purpose. Here you are considering what you will need to bring every day in all that you do and who you are being through your leadership behaviour.

Our own example of this is of course our dream about 4i. A few years ago we created a vision about what could emerge and what difference it might make. But we had to fuel our dream with an everyday resolve and as a result we researched, wrote, networked and created the foundation for this ground-breaking approach. Not every step led to success but we grappled tirelessly to clarify our thinking and within a year we found ourselves being invited into organisations to talk about transformational leadership and 4i. And as we had hoped and imagined this led to our working with leaders and teams and helping them have those essential conversations that make such a difference to how people work and succeed together.

You now have the key components for your leadership map and this is one of the most powerful enablers for shaping your action, your behaviour and your vision. Our simple encouragement is to put it all together on the page following so that it captures the spirit of your imagination.

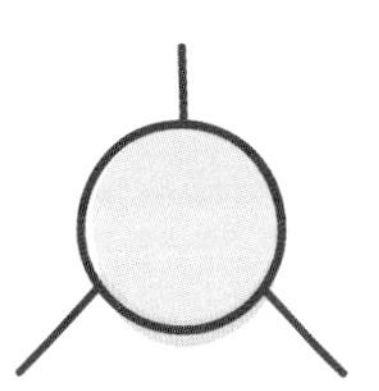

Complete your personal Leadership Map

What matters most to me?

My core values

My best beliefs

What impact do I want to have on others?

What reputation do I want to build that would make me proud?

What's my dream and cause?

The purpose and commitment I will need is...

IN SUMMARY

This chapter was about:

- Daring to dream
- Developing your personal leadership map
- Bringing purpose to your dream

So, what are you going to do with your one wild and precious life? Your dream will need all the hope, imagination and purpose that you can provide to help it live. Dreams also challenge the current reality and in the next chapter we will talk about how you can share your dream and ignite a spark in others.

Ignite

From the little spark may burst a mighty flame

Dante

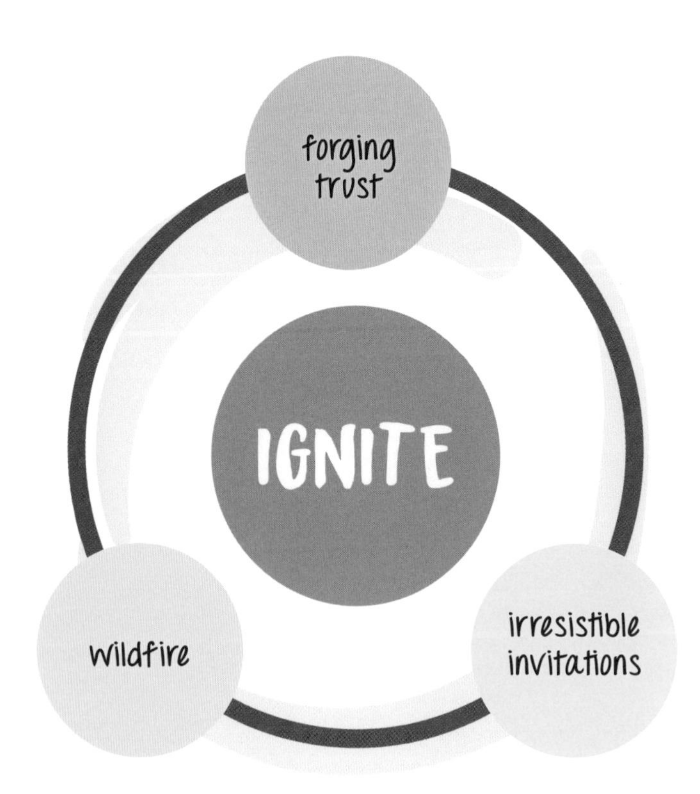
forging trust
IGNITE
wildfire
irresistible invitations

Ignite

This chapter is about igniting enthusiasm and inviting others. Once you've imagined a bigger and better future it's then up to you to build trust and excitement in the hearts and minds of others and fan those flames until they catch alight.

Ignite is all about connection and we are already wired for it. We are social beings. It's one of the most bewildering of realities that we spend so much time at work, frequently in teams, and yet often know so little about each other. This isn't because we don't like our colleagues but because, inexplicably, we conclude that work doesn't have much to do with real relationships. The opposite is true. We need each other. We need to share our energy and ideas. We need people to value and care for us. We need people to help us, give us courage and encourage us when we lose faith.

So how then, if we are wired in this way, do we build deeper connections with one another? We do it by having personal and purposeful conversations. Such conversations build trust and ignite possibility and belief. They ignite fires. In this chapter we will explore:

1. How to forge trust
2. How to make irresistible invitations
3. How to spread ideas and belief like wildfire

Forging trust

The inability to open up to hope is what blocks trust, and blocked trust is the reason for blighted dreams

Elizabeth Gilbert

We've found over the years that trust is critical for people in organisations. However, trust is something that we rarely see on the agenda when teams meet together. Take the following findings from a few recent reports on trust that underline its importance to leaders.

- In a survey of 33,000 respondents across 28 countries, Edelman's Trust Barometer found that trust in business had fallen to 43%.
- Harvard Business Review reports that in organisations with high trust there is 74% less stress, 106% more energy, 50% higher productivity, 13% fewer sick days, 76% more engagement, 29% more satisfaction and 40% less burnout.
- Leadership IQ reports that 44% of people strongly distrust their top management. A further 36% only have moderate trust in their leaders.
- PWC reports that 55% of CEOs think that a lack of trust is a threat to their organisation's growth.

These figures are stark and begin to explain why trust regularly comes up as a leadership issue in the workplace.

To ignite a flame in others it's important to pay attention to trust and trustworthiness. Trust defines our relationships. In trusting relationships we speak openly, ask for help and accept challenges. In non-trusting relationships cynicism, defensiveness and anxiety prevail.

Where employees don't think their leaders look out for them then trust is low. And lack of trust correlates to low productivity and lack of motivation. When there is deeper trust between leaders and employees everyone feels enabled to take a risk and go further. So how do you build trust?

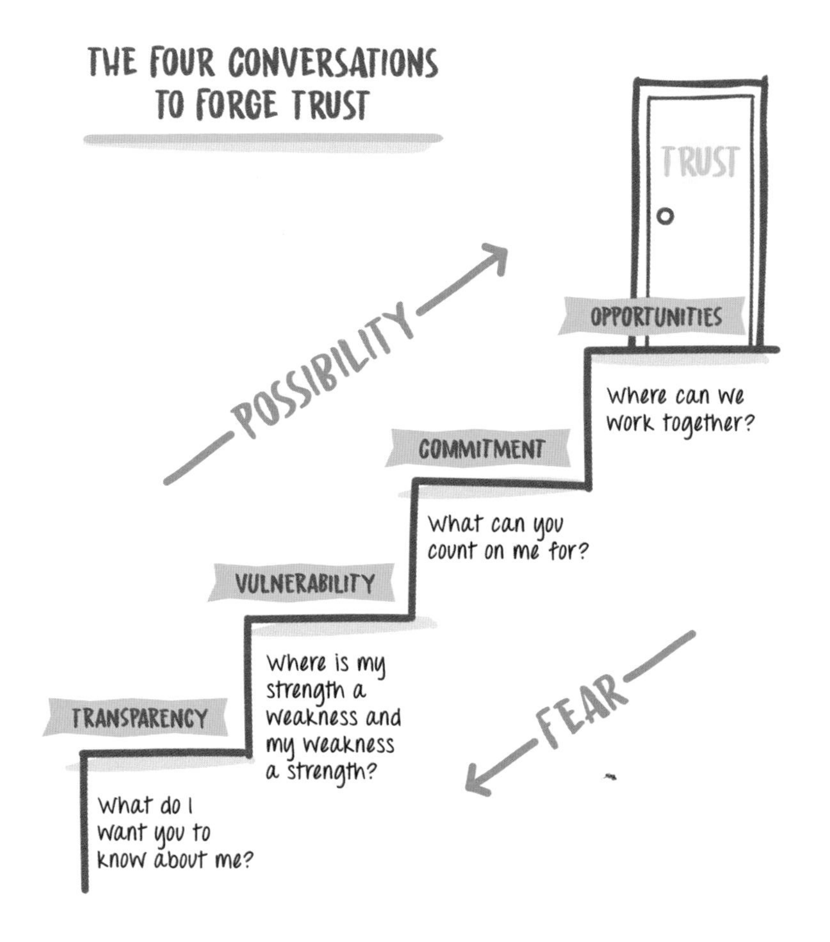

Let's take Joni's case as an example of what can go wrong when you ignore trust!

Joni is an MD with a fierce determination to succeed. She is fast-moving and visionary and she certainly knows how to interrupt. But despite her charisma, when we first met Joni she wasn't getting people to buy into her vision; and when we investigated further we heard story after story from people down the line that they didn't trust her or her top team.

Telling Joni this news didn't go down well. She was impatient with the 'nay-sayers' as she referred to them. They just didn't like the change that she was driving, she explained. But in all the surveys the same message was coming through. Trust in leadership was poor.

When we dug a little deeper we saw why. The problem was that while Joni was inspirational she was also inconsistent. This showed up in the way she let bad behaviour among her colleagues go unchallenged; and she also had her favourites, which left some people feeling she wasn't even-handed. So although her message about values and good behaviour was clear, what employees saw was that what really mattered to Joni was results – at any cost. And this left people feeling disheartened and disengaged.

What did Joni need to address? It was clear that trust was the big issue and we created this approach to forging trust for exactly such situations. It addresses not only the essential building blocks of trust but also highlights the key questions that allow us to access a much deeper relationship with others.

Trust begins and ends with the conversations we are prepared to have with others – but before we start talking to other people let's take a step back and remember that our mindset is critical.

Our *fearful mindset* will stop us from taking a risk. Our limiting beliefs about ourselves and others will act as a brake and make us cautious. We won't dare to open up. We will look for reasons to leave things the way they are. Our *possibility mindset* on the other hand will remind us that far more can be achieved when we are deeply linked up with others. With possibility we take risks, we explore and we bring a deeper commitment to our relationships.

So pause for a moment and get in touch with your creative sense of possibility. Align yourself behind it and make it your intent. And now think about the following four conversations that will accelerate and help you build trusting relationships.

1. Transparency: 'what do I want you to know about me?'

The first conversation with others that will help forge trust and safety is transparency. Transparency is about removing our mask and letting people know who we are and what our agenda is. It's also about revealing our intent, our hope and our willingness to be open. It includes having the courage to be honest and let others in.

We can all think of examples of times when we've shared something important or confidential with someone and been let down. Such breakdowns can end relationships and create deep scars that last for a lifetime. Yet if we listen to our fears we will get nowhere. If we want to build trust we have to be prepared to choose our *possibility mindset* again, not naively, but with openness and a readiness to share what matters most to us.

2. Vulnerability: 'where is my strength a weakness and my weakness a strength?'

The second conversation on vulnerability is about being emotionally available and not pretending that we're good at everything. It's about letting others see our human fallibility.

When we raise the topic of vulnerability with leaders they often visibly flinch. In their understanding of the word it can be seen as a weakness. As the leading thinker on vulnerability, Brene Brown says: '*When we spend our lives waiting until we're perfect or bulletproof we ultimately sacrifice relationships and opportunities that may not be recoverable.'*

In other words, when we are looking to build trust it's important that we accept our imperfection and stop believing we need to have all the answers. Instead we need to ask for support, it helps us, invites people closer and has them feel valued. And when people feel valued they then share more of their ideas and insights, which open up new possibilities.

When we are vulnerable in this way it matters far less when we falter. In trusting relationships faltering is a given – it's the getting back up and moving forward with the help of others that matters.

Such robust relationships are essential as we build our understanding of one another and lean more into those issues that we can't always tackle alone.

3. Commitment: 'What can you count on me for?'

The first two conversations inevitably lead on to what level of commitment we have for each other. This is a conversation about integrity and what people can rely on you for. There is a key difference here between what we agree to and what we commit to. Commitment is built on being true to our word. It's a contract that we have with another person. It's our promise to be reliable and to follow through. When leaders don't walk their talk this is precisely where they are seen as failing in their commitment. Having a robust conversation about commitment is an essential foundation for forging any trusting relationship.

4. Opportunity: 'Where can we work together?'

And finally, because we now know what really matters to each other, we can look for those exciting and stretching opportunities that will cement and enhance our relationship.

When we take opportunities we do so in the full knowledge that we will support one another. We will take risks and embark on bold pieces of new work together. We will share insights and information that previously we kept to ourselves. We reach out to each other at a much deeper level than we have dared before and become champions for each other. Trust is forged in our intent and with the belief that it's possible to create something better between people. By taking opportunities to work together we create a greater sense of belonging, better teamworking and vastly improve our chances of success.

In all these four conversations we ignite trust. Having such open dialogue generates the feeling that someone 'has our back' and fosters the sense of togetherness that is so essential to life. This is a deeply affirming experience and it can make us feel unstoppable. And it's at this point that we really start to accelerate and build the belief that together, with others, we can tackle any challenge.

CHOOSE NOW

- **Where do you see a need for more trust in your life?**
- **What new level of transparency, vulnerability and commitment are you prepared to bring?**
- **Commit now to having a conversation with someone where forging trust will make a big difference**

As you start to think about forging trust it's also helpful to look beyond the person or people you might be wanting to build a relationship with and think about the topics you find difficult to talk about. The model overleaf helps outline the levels of trust or distrust that can be experienced in conversation.

Trust is also topic dependent

Trust

- *Full partnership* is where you work together, share ideas, disagree robustly and fully commit to each other. Success is shared and problems are solved without blame.
- *Actively seeking out* is where you go out of your way to approach others for their ideas and input. You want people to challenge and support you.
- *Curiosity* comes when you understand that you do not have the full picture. You are interested in exploring other perspectives. You want to know what other people think.
- *Welcoming* feels like an openness to others. You don't want to be on your own and you invite the relationship conversation.

Distrust

- *Avoidance* shows up in your turning away from others. You avoid this person or the conversation and are not interested in their views and thoughts.
- *Judgemental* behaviour comes from holding fixed views. You are not open to challenge. Everything you hear about the topic under discussion is filtered through a negative bias.
- *Active distrust* often shows up when you are looking for hidden motives, when you bring negativity to conversations or even share your dark suspicions about the other person behind their back.
- *Hostility* is present when your level of trust is so low that you are thinking about or even working to 'bring the other person down'. Their failure feels like your success.

LEVELS OF TRUST

PASSIVITY ------------------- PASSIVITY

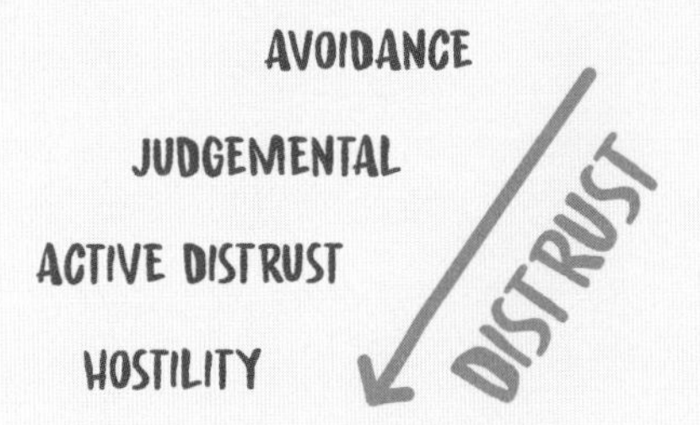

NOTICE NOW

- Who are the key people you're working with and what topics are you dealing with?
- What level of trust do you have with them on these topics?

We all have conversations we find difficult. We hope that it will be rare that you go as far as hostility but in our coaching and team work we do know how triggered people sometimes get! The challenge here, however, is to accept that some of your conversations will be difficult both in and out of work. Try not to let time pass and hope that the difficulty will go away. The truth is that when we don't face into conversations we erode trust. So make it your practice to become aware of awkward topics and find ways to make them more open and more constructive.

Irresistible invitations

A cynic is a passionate person who does not want to be disappointed again. And the secret is not to speak to a person's cynicism, but to speak to their passion

Ben Zander

With a foundation of trust you can now think about igniting the passion, excitement and commitment in others so that they want to come with you. The focus here is to make an invitation that is so powerful it becomes irresistible. No surprise that such an invitation requires passion and belief.

Joni had a task on her hands. We started by helping her build trust in her top team but the underlying issue hadn't gone away. She was leading a business that was currently very profitable but really needed to innovate. 'We are very successful today and yet we have never been so close to the edge' she said. Joni saw that her team were tolerating inefficient business practices, such as command and control management, that were holding the organisation back.

She had started to imagine how things could be very different. It was clear to her that she needed to lead a big change in culture to help the company face the future – one where people took more ownership, felt more empowered and brought more innovation to their work. However, the challenge she faced was that some of her colleagues really liked the old way of doing things and were resistant to change. They couldn't see what was wrong. Why meddle with something that wasn't broken?

Undeterred, Joni sat down with her senior team and shared her observations and her vision for the future. She made an irresistible invitation.

To make an irresistible invitation there is a strong requirement for personal authenticity and vulnerability. You have to bring your personal belief, be genuine in your interest in people and be willing to be aspirational. Here are the essential qualities that we believe make invitations compelling.

Meet people where they are

Meet people where they are – not where you are. In essence, listen to what people have to say. Build curiosity and leave people feeling as though they really matter.

There is one straightforward guideline here – start being much more curious about what other people want. Ask questions to which you don't know the answers. Listen hard and generously. And be prepared to go off-piste because that might be much more interesting.

The model opposite can help you think about how to meet people where they are. Are they ready now or do they need to be further engaged? Once you know where they are starting from then you can adapt your conversation to their circumstances.

Remember, even though you want them to join up with you it is also vital that you are genuinely interested in what they want too. What will they get out of your invitation? If you can create the conditions for their success then you will have every chance of building momentum.

Be truthful

People crave leaders who are real and authentic. This means telling the truth and showing that it matters to you. You can also build trust more easily when you are completely honest about the current reality and the impact it's having.

Many leaders say they are looking to go from 'good to great' when in fact they are going from 'awful to ok' and everyone knows it. So remember to tell people *where* you are starting from, your part in the current reality, and *why* we need to change. Tell them where they're already exceptional. Be clear about what needs interrupting and outline the consequences of staying still. Speak to people not from the safety of your role but rather as someone who is committed to building something with their help.

Tell a compelling story

Because leadership is personal, telling your story sits at the heart of ignition. Your story encapsulates everything in your leadership map, what matters to you and the journey you are taking people on. You simply have to share it in a compelling way.

So tell people what you stand for and why and what has shaped your values and beliefs. Tell them about your purpose and the difference your dream might make. Show that you care, that you want their input and that you need them to come with you.

You have to help people feel it's their journey as well as yours so that they feel you are inviting their full contribution in terms of ideas, energy and commitment. Remember what we've just talked about concerning trust building – that's the spirit of partnership you are looking for.

Ask for help

The best leaders always ask for help. They know that they can't make things happen on their own. And when you ask for help make sure you mean it. Leave people in no doubt – it is their participation that you are inviting here. And their help will make all the difference to your dream.

When you make an invitation you will find that people respond in very different ways. Some will respond readily and be willing to engage immediately in a conversation about possibility. Others will be resistant and argue vehemently for the status quo.

This is a challenge that you need to be ready to face. You may be crystal clear about the opportunities and challenges, and your own optimism and energy may be high, but before you even get started you may encounter serious resistance.

Meeting resistance was exactly the case for Joni who, just to remind you, was looking to introduce innovative ways of working into her team and organisation. She had to be unambiguous and resolved about what was at stake. She had to talk about the current situation and what she thought would happen if the change did or did not occur. She was also clear that she needed the full support and backing of those around her and it was important to declare her complete commitment for the journey ahead. The train, she said, was leaving the station, and everyone had a choice as to whether to get on board.

Being truthful and declaring this threshold is essential for leaders. The future must be inspiring enough, the invitation must be powerful enough and the leader must be looking for a genuine spirit of possibility to emerge. But people also need to know they have a choice to make.

In this respect you are making a statement of intent and people have to decide whether they want to be part of this future or move onto something more suited to their own ambitions.

Don't be surprised if some people don't come with you but those who choose to will be fully on board. When you have crossed this threshold then your conversations are likely to be characterised by enthusiasm and bold thinking. However, at the same time, you and the team might find fear takes hold and the challenges look daunting. This is to be expected and can happen when you leave the safety and comfort of home. Big goals when viewed from today's reality often look unreasonable. Your task at this point is to remind your team that while it might take them some time to reach the destination you believe it is both essential and achievable.

This means building trust and commitment and talking about how you will all act with integrity. It also means looking for opportunities to work together and celebrating every success as you look to build confidence and belief.

How to make an irresistible invitation

Meet people where they are

Before you get started be curious about:

- What people are currently experiencing and the stories they are telling
- How much trust they currently have in you
- What their hopes and dreams are and the difference they want to make

Be truthful

Authenticity is critical here so use the following as a guide and be completely unambiguous about:

- The current reality and everyone's contribution to it
- What we are tolerating, where we are exceptional, and the consequences of both
- Is your dream and the change it requires optional?

Tell a compelling story

This is where you breathe life into your dream so be prepared to put yourself out there.

- Talk openly about who you are, what has shaped you and why this matters to you.
- Bring to life your dream and tell stories from the future, paint a picture with words about what you can imagine.
- Bring to life how this would affect what we're doing today. Make it relevant to your audience. Let them know what's in it for them.

Ask for help

This may be the most important part of your invitation so be transparent and vulnerable

- Ask people how they can make your dream a reality.
- Ask them what you've missed and if they can help you make it bigger and better.
- Ask them to be part of something that will make a difference

These first steps are critical for the journey on which you are embarking. When there is purpose in actions and alignment in team behaviour then progress is assured.

CHOOSE NOW

- **Work out who you need to ignite and how to meet them where they are.**
- **What is the invitation you want to make and how will you make it irresistible?**
- **What is the impact you want to see as a result?**

Wildfire

An irresistible invitation can spread like wildfire

When great ideas take hold they can spread quickly across boundaries. Joni had ignited a spark in her own team and others soon wanted to join up with her. Her ideas were contagious and began to spread like wildfire. Big ideas need to be helped along. This is how you can help them to spread.

Be ready to build momentum

When you are guided by your dream and behaving in line with your values you will find that you have a magnetic attraction to others. There is something compelling when you lead with integrity. Others will want to be involved with you. They will feel drawn by your energy and focus. And with their enthusiasm you will create even more momentum.

Claire, a wonderful client we work with, told us she knew this was happening when a fellow director came up to her after an annual conference and asked 'what have you been doing with your people? Something about them is completely different and I'd like to get the same energy into my team.' Claire was delighted to be approached in this way. She was deeply committed to making people across the whole organisation feel that they could make more impact and she was more than willing to share her insights. Importantly, she left her colleague feeling that it would be great if they could make a further difference together, and it is exactly this sharing of intention that underpins wildfire.

Be resilient

Sometimes your dream will be challenged. There will be times when the voices of cynics and doubters will emerge. At these times your resilience will be watched and judged. Some people will look out for evidence that change can't occur. They will be pleased by your setbacks. But surprisingly you will also have people just waiting to join up with you and if you show that you can navigate setbacks then this inspires confidence.

In our work we've seen that people don't just want idealistic leaders who have vision but no substance. They want committed leaders who keep bringing belief whatever short-term difficulties they might encounter. They want leaders who face into difficult conversations. And they want leaders who also ask for support from others because they know they can't succeed on their own.

Ignite energy in others

A while ago we met a CEO who told us that he would judge success by the amount of energy running through his organisation. If there was more at the end of his tenure than there was when he first took office then he would know he'd done a good job.

In effect, this CEO was talking about wildfire – the leadership that spreads when they feel purposeful and passionate. When such energy flows then people, teams and organisations thrive. So how do you ignite energy in others? Here are a few ways to begin.

- Physical energy – Urge people to make a difference. Point to opportunities still to be taken.
- Intellectual energy – Provide evidence of success. Create and share road maps that help people see where further success can be achieved.
- Emotional energy – Encourage collaboration wherever possible. Forge trust and highlight and celebrate joy.
- Spiritual energy – Build belief and purpose by consistently talking to the dream and cause.

Be willing to let go

Possibilities are unlimited if you don't care who gets the credit

When you want wildfire it's essential to let go. This can feel dangerous because it's your dream and you don't want it to be corrupted or diluted. But you have to let people own it for themselves.

Carlos was a Brazilian leader who had been working in Europe for a global engineering company. A few years ago he and his team had implemented a change to customer service that was transforming the business. He had ignited a dream in his area and suddenly his colleagues wanted a part of it. This was a great accolade for Carlos but he wasn't entirely happy about it. Why? Because his colleagues wanted to do things in their way – not his way.

It wasn't easy for Carlos to let people take hold of his idea. He felt he was losing control but then he had an epiphany. Their success was his success. All he needed to do was remember that he had set the train in motion. Where it went and who would drive it wasn't important. What mattered was that he'd been the catalyst.

In other words, wildfire is created when everyone feels ownership.

CHOOSE NOW

- Where can you see potential for wildfire to spread?
- Invite someone in and give them the opportunity to make your idea their own.

IN SUMMARY

This chapter was about:

- Forging trust
- Irresistible invitations
- Wildfire

So you now have a set of tools and perspectives that will help you to ignite the spark of people's excitement into a mighty flame! What happens next is to consider how that energy and belief can be channelled in order to make the biggest possible difference to people's work and life.

Impact

Every now and then, someone arrives in your life and changes everything, and you can barely remember what it was like before.

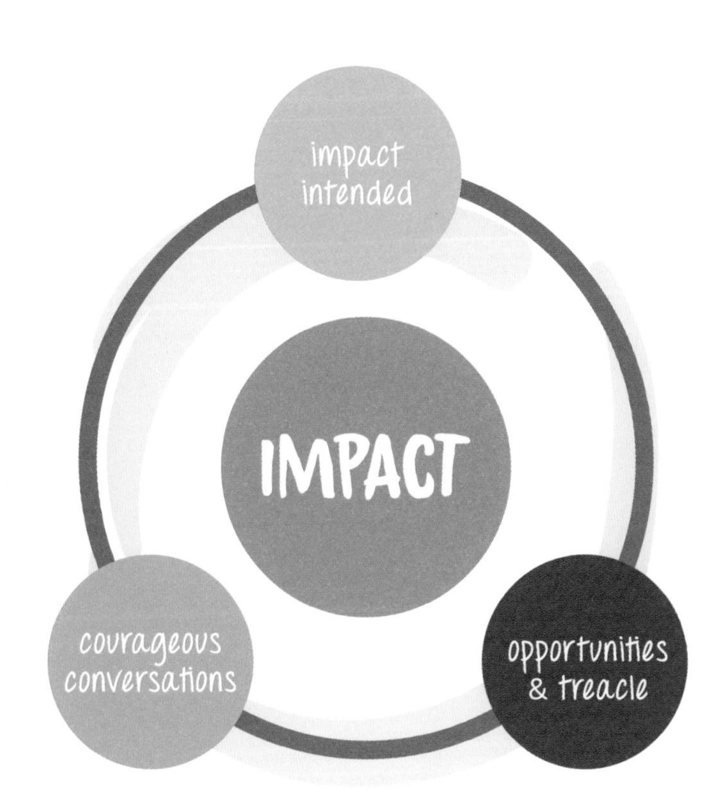
impact
intended
IMPACT
courageous
conversations
opportunities
& treacle

Impact

So far we've talked about Interrupt, Imagine and Ignite, the three phases of 4i Leadership that help you prepare for Impact. This is the moment where you commit to action and where your leadership starts to transform those things that matter most to you.

In this chapter we will look at how you can take what you've noticed, explored and imagined throughout 4i and use it to create the impact you want, wherever you want. Given this we believe there are three places to focus on that will give you the best chance of making the difference you want.

1. Ensuring the impact you intend is the impact felt
2. Seizing opportunities and tackling treacle
3. Having courageous conversations

Impact intended

Why would anyone want to be led by you?

As leaders we are often blisfully unaware or wilfully blind to the impact that we are having. And this all comes down to our personal awareness.

In how many areas of work and life can we say that the impact we intend to have is actually the impact we want? Most of us want to lead in an engaging way – the way described in our leadership map – and we will all have achieved this at times. But we will also surely remember occasions when instead of leaving people feeling inspired we've left them feeling confused, frustrated or alienated instead – when that was clearly not our intention.

This aspect of leadership is fascinating for anyone who wants to make a big difference and it leads us to investigate how 'feedforward' is such a critical tool in helping leaders stay at the top of their game.

Why do we use the term feedforward rather than feedback? We do so because it helps instill the notion that what emboldens us are the constructive and forward-looking reflections of colleagues who tell us their truth about how they experience our leadership.

Receiving such unambiguous feedforward is rare and it requires people to be honest with us, to be trustworthy and to be absolutely committed to our growth and success. Importantly here we are asking people to tell us not only what qualities we bring but, vitally, what impact it has on them when we bring these qualities.

To get the benefit of feedforward it's also essential that we listen to what is said and that means both the good and the bad. Interestingly, most people have a negative bias. We treat positive input like Teflon – it just slides straight off us and we lose it. And we treat negative input like Velcro – they stick fast to us and we find them hard to get rid of.

To counter this it is helpful to see all feedforward as information that builds awareness of our impact. In this respect feedforward can be most powerful when looked at through the following three conversations. And we refer to these as conversations because feedforward such as this is always an opportunity to talk, clear up misunderstandings and make adjustments to how we work together.

Our belief about feedforward is as follows – if one person tells you something you should always listen, if more than two people tell you the same thing then listen harder, and if everyone around you gives you the same reflections it's either the truth or a conspiracy! Here's where to start:

1. The acknowledgement conversation

How easy is it to enjoy the person you've already become?

Just how good are you? This may feel an immodest or even an awkward question to ask but leaders who want to make an impact need to know how powerful they already are. And we are not talking about how successful you are here. Rather we are talking about the human qualities that you bring when you are 100% all-in and that underpins your impact. Here are a few examples of the human qualities that can be present when people are making a significant leadership impact:

Of course some people find it awkward to acknowledge that these qualities matter so much. As one rather pained leader, Graham, said to us 'I thought this leadership coaching was going to be about all the projects that I've got on. I didn't think it was going to be so much about me?'

Graham had started to realise something important. He had seen that his leadership impact had less to do with what he was doing and more to do with how he was showing up. Sometimes he showed up in a way that inspired other people – and sometimes he didn't.

What made Graham thoughtful was that he hadn't previously recognised this difference. He thought he was pretty much the same every day. And that people responded to him in pretty much the same way too. But the feedforward he got from his peers and team told a very different story.

When you are fully committed, his colleagues told him, you are inclusive, inviting and buzzing with energy. It's great to be involved in projects with you and you leave us feeling very special. At such times we feel lucky to know you and be led by you.

This was great insight for Graham but he was quick to deflect it. 'It's all a bit embarrassing,' he said, 'and they probably feel that they have to say nice things about me.'

This is such a typical response from leaders. It's as though they have been conditioned only to measure success by results. And yet it's a kind of profound poetry for people when they accept the wonderful qualities they have.

We have great fun with our clients in this territory – helping them to get better at acknowledging themselves.

Helping people to own and declare out loud what they are already really good at – and how great it makes other people feel – makes many of them squirm. We often find clients to be absurdly modest and sometimes they downright refuse to admit that there is anything positive to say about themselves. 'I'm really not very good at anything' they cry. But we know this isn't true and we remind them that at the very least other people must believe in them or how else would they have reached the position they are in?

So we challenge them to accept praise, both so that they feel better about themselves and because they can then model the self-belief that they would want the people around them to have.

2. The encouragement conversation

We are all better than we think we are

Where can you step up? Acknowledging our strengths is vital and it underpins our confidence. However, it's also important to get feedforward from people about where we can do and be even better.

Having someone who is totally enrolled in us, and committed to telling the truth about where we fall short or can step up, can be extraordinarily reassuring. Note here that the encouragement we are talking about isn't criticism. It's aiming at helping us be even more successful. Such encouragement emboldens us.

Kathy was a client who asked for coaching because she believed in support and challenge. She was surprised, however, by the first question we asked. 'Just how much of yourself are you prepared to risk here?'

The immediate encouragement to Kathy was to think big, be ambitious and not hold back and she immediately engaged in a conversation about what this might mean for her. Did she sometimes hold back? Of course. Was the coaching there to help her be absolutely brilliant? Yes. But this also meant encouraging Kathy to get out of her comfort zone and start taking a few well-judged risks.

3. The 'watch out' conversation

You really need to know that some of what you do isn't working!

Where do you get in your own way? Whether we like it or not we all have blind spots and we can all benefit from understanding what these are. Even when we are aiming to be at our best there are still traps we fall into. This is normal and it's not intentional, we just don't notice the impact we sometimes have when we behave in this way. And when we don't notice, the behaviour can become a habit. This starts to be a big problem when our impact reduces other people's energy, confidence and ability.

So you really need to know when some of what you are doing isn't working. And feedforward is incredibly useful here.

David is a leader who is super bright, knows what matters to him and sometimes comes over as extremely arrogant. At his best he stimulates people with his thinking and insights but at other times he just gets righteous and preachy and at these times he provokes division and frustration. As a senior leader it's so easy for David to take over and dominate any meeting he is in. And when he does so nobody else dares to offer an alternative view or dares to be creative. This of course is not the impact David wants!

Understanding that this is the unintended impact he sometimes has means David can now 'watch out' for this trap. And significantly he has also invited people in his own team to give him a signal when he is being over-dominant so that he can adjust his behaviour accordingly.

These three conversations are not always easy. If we are truly committed to being the best leader we can be then we have to invite a bolder conversation. The fearful mindset doesn't want to know. The possibility mindset is endlessly curious and optimistic.

CHOOSE NOW

Go and ask two or three people who you trust to give their honest and constructive feedforward to the following questions

The acknowledgement conversation

- What do you really value about my leadership?
- When I'm at my best what impact does this have on you?

The encouragement conversation

- What do I need to start or do more of?
- What would the impact be if I did this?

The 'watch out' conversation

- What are my blind spots that get in the way?
- And what impact do these blind spots have on you?

With this information what new choices will you make?

Opportunities and treacle

We are continually faced with great opportunities, brilliantly disguised as unsolvable problems

Margaret Mead

We're now going to explore two key ways we can make an even bigger impact. How to seize the opportunities that will make the biggest difference and how to tackle the treacle that often causes our best endeavours to stall and falter.

How to take the opportunities and tackle the frustrations are things that always come up in our work. And unpacking what they mean and finding ways to look at them is extraordinarily potent. Our simple way of looking at this helps leaders to get to grips with these issues.

We often see committed people getting bogged down because they're too busy, too distracted and too stressed to see and seize the opportunities in front of them. Alternatively, they are too tired or cynical to tackle the difficulties they face. This is a real shame because the opportunities around them and the treacle they're wading through could make the biggest difference to what they're trying to do. Whenever we ask people to explore this their energy grows, closely followed by a whole raft of possibilities. When you're looking to make a significant impact and are up to something big, these conversations act like oxygen.

Seize the opportunities

Every adventure means leaving the safety of home

Katie, a senior executive in retail, works in an organisation where there are a lot of politics. This is not uncommon. It hasn't been easy for her but she has a cause that she is passionate about – and that cause is gender equality at work.

For some time Katie felt frustrated. She had hoped and believed that the change she wanted would be led by the organisation. The time had surely come! But after some powerful feedforward from colleagues she realised that it was up to her to seize the opportunity and make it her responsibility to create awareness and action around this most fundamental of issues. So Katie, inspired by possibility, and backed by a growing number of colleagues, staked her personal reputation on speaking, writing and engaging people in her vision.

This was a huge step for her and it took real courage. But because she is passionate and visionary Katie took her first step and ignited the enthusiasm of hundreds of colleagues.

Just six months after starting her campaign Katie saw tangible results. The topic was on the boardroom agenda. Managers had the issue at the forefront of their minds and, best of all, more women were being appointed across the organisation into senior jobs. As Katie reflected, 'looking back it seems astonishing that it took us so long to seize an opportunity that affected so many people'.

The message here is a simple one. Don't wait for others to lead the change you want to see. Seize the opportunity to make a difference. Look for people who want to join up with you and speak up.

At first glance such opportunities need little explanation. They are clearly those openings which lead to benefit or payback. But look more closely and there are different sorts of opportunity that require different investment from you. We refer to these different types of opportunity as open goals, big bets and hidden treasure.

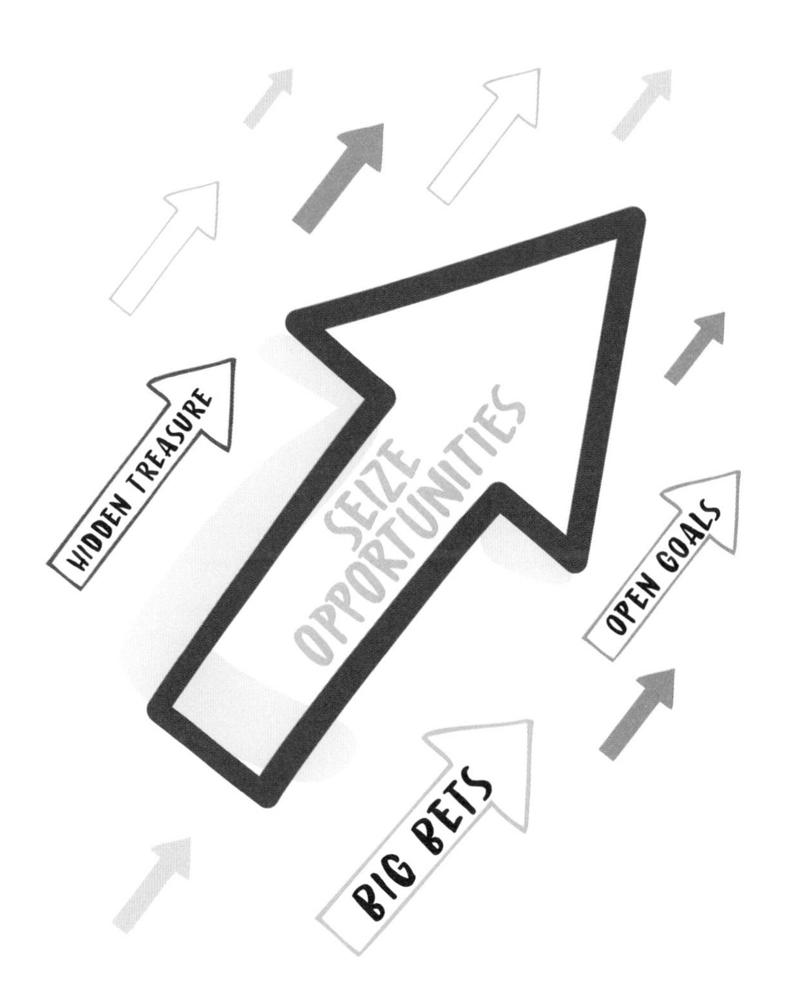
HIDDEN TREASURE
SEIZE
OPPORTUNITIES
OPEN GOALS
BIG BETS

Open Goals are those opportunities that are just waiting to be taken by you. They are the quick wins, the slam dunks. Surprisingly, however, we don't always see our open goals. People around us can often see them better than we can.

Open goals give us immediate opportunities. We need to be clear about what advantages they offer and we might need focus and courage to score them, but open goals give us the chance to get on the front foot, create momentum and build success.

Big Bets are those opportunities where there's a prize to be won even though the outcome isn't guaranteed. With big bets there is a risk involved, so we have to be bold. Furthermore, big bets only pay back when we invest something of ourselves, our energy or our resources. When we make this sort of commitment we generate excitement, possibility and purpose. Big bets can make a real difference to people who want to join something where the potential rewards are high.

Hidden Treasure is an opportunity waiting to be discovered. With hidden treasure we know there's something out there that might be game changing but we have to go out of our way to find it. There's no reliable map here; instead we get glimpses of it or hear rumours of its whereabouts. It might be found in new research or in new technology. It might be predicted in new markets or product development. It might be discovered in a new collaboration.

Hidden treasure also hints at the possibility and opportunity for something rewarding and exciting to emerge. Its value may be unknowable and that is part of the allure. A large part of the opportunity here lies in creating desire and appetite for adventure.

Each of these three openings into opportunity requires optimism and belief. But, as ever, that may not be enough. 'Going for it' also requires that you be prepared to leave behind those things with which you have grown comfortable. Action is necessary but there may be losses to bear as well as gains to be made.

How to surface new opportunities

How do you recognise the opportunities that are waiting for you? Unsurprisingly, these become clearer when you are open and engaging others in forward-looking conversations.

1. What does an open goal, a big bet or hidden treasure look like for you? How big can you think? Is this informed by your dream, something that needs *interrupting*, or both?
2. Once you have identified an opportunity explore it for a while and think about the difference it could make. See how it might speak to some of your inspiration from *imagine*.
3. Who are you likely to be working alongside? What's in it for them? Who will you need to build relationships with and *ignite*?
4. Identify how to start. When we start looking at opportunities they can feel awkward or daunting. Keep it simple and think of the first step you can take to bring that opportunity to life.
5. Be bold. Tell others about the opportunity and above all get on the front foot and start a bolder conversation.

NOTICE NOW

- What does leaving the safety of home look like for you?
- What are the open goals you can see in front of you?
- What are the big bets you can see ahead?
- Where do you have a feeling or a sense for hidden treasure?

Tackle the treacle

What are the issues that refuse to go away?

It's always possible to make a difference by seizing opportunities. But the other lens that is critical to use in making an impact is to see where you can tackle the treacle.

Treacle can be identified by looking at those questions that refuse to go away. All organisations have them. They are things that make no sense and frustrate us. We call them elephants, taboos and inconvenient truths. Jonathan, a great friend and colleague, calls them 'the nonsense' – because when they're exposed to the cold light of day, they make no sense! We call it treacle because it's sticky and wading through it impedes the progress of much that we're trying to accomplish. The problem with treacle is that it slows us down and costs us time, money and belief. Indeed it's this treacle that saps energy, triggers our fear and causes many of our best dreams, ideas and plans to fail.

Elephants are big issues and open secrets that are always in the way. Everyone knows about them and yet everyone dances around them. They are too big and difficult to handle so we ignore them or pretend they aren't there. Surprisingly, when we leave them long enough elephants even become invisible – they can become an accepted part of the culture.

Taboos are dangerous issues. Don't talk about them unless you want to make yourself a pariah! Sometimes taboo subjects are so deeply ingrained that we aren't even conscious of them. So we learn to avoid particular conversations and we go nowhere near sensitive territory – even though we don't really know why. Newcomers learn instinctively to avoid taboos and also learn not to ask too many questions about them.

Inconvenient truths are the things we pretend not to know. At a personal level these might be our lazy habits or small-minded behaviours. It's inconvenient of course that flying contributes to climate change – but what else can we do when we want to holiday abroad?

In organisations, inconvenient truths are also pervasive and may include going along with bad practices and processes that clearly don't work. Performance management is an interesting example that often comes up in these conversations.

We know we really ought to address inconvenient truths but to tackle them requires us to make a radical change. So instead we put up with them or turn a blind eye even though we know we are storing up problems for the future.

All these forms of treacle are present in life. We have treacle at home and certainly at work. Whenever things feel overcomplicated, hard work or just make no sense, then you can be sure treacle is at work. If you focus on it then you can work out just how big a problem it causes and you can choose to do something about it.

We've noticed that treacle is really easy to find. Everyone knows about it and it takes no time at all to get this conversation going in workshops. It is the single biggest factor that gets in the way of everything leaders are trying to do. Leaders who commit to eliminating treacle have the best chance of helping their people to move quicker and be brilliant. Treacle may not be easy to shift, but if you manage to reduce or eliminate it then the positive impact that has on people and results is phenomenal. In contrast, leaders who ignore treacle can only be sure that they are placing discretionary effort, possibility and success at risk.

NOTICE NOW

- What are the issues that refuse to go away?
- What's your usual response to treacle?
- What gets in the way that you always work around?
- What do you encourage others not to talk about?
- What do you turn a blind eye to because it feels it's too difficult to address?

Breaking the silence – a way to tackle the treacle

When we dare to break that silence we allow everyone to do their best thinking – Margaret Heffernan

We've all worked in, and experienced, organisations and teams where there is distrust, where there is little alignment on the way forward and where poor working practices prevail. In other words, where treacle is holding us back.

In these circumstances it's especially valuable to encourage people to challenge and disagree. Why? Because disagreement is healthy. Indeed, supressing conflict stifles creativity, ensures that nothing changes and usually creates more treacle. So instead of glossing over problems, leaders need to help their teams face into them.

So why is disagreement so difficult? Many people of course fear and avoid conflict. We associate conflict with arguments and fights, winners and losers. Conflict itself then becomes an elephant or even a taboo.

In daring to disagree we focus not on the people involved but on the topic at stake. And when we become practised at disagreement it allows us to consider a full range of options.

Jenny was a leader in a new role who quickly recognised that her new team were very risk-averse. They never disagreed and always went along with each other even when it was clear that they had different opinions. As a result there was no spark in the team and Jenny was frustrated. How could she help her people to constructively disagree with one another?

Jenny raised this concern with her team and after some prompting they agreed it was treacle. Then, with some trepidation, they agreed to work on it together.

As we started this intervention the room was tense – so to begin with we established a few ground rules:

1. This is a safe place to explore the issue. Try pushing your own boundaries. There will be no recriminations.
2. The intent is not to be right but to bring different options to the table.
3. Think of this conversation as a way to understand each other's points of view. Listen hard.
4. Allow yourself to enjoy the energy that gets released when you disagree with others.
5. Adopt a *possibility* mindset throughout and especially keep it in mind when you challenge others and get challenged yourself.
6. Keep your input to the issue and not the person. Don't make those who have different opinions to you 'wrong'.

The topic we chose to start with was a new change programme – a contentious issue that we knew divided opinions. And to start the exercise we split the team into two groups and asked them to prepare for a 'no-holds barred' debate where they took opposing positions.

We then initiated a 20-minute session where each group was encouraged to speak with passion and say things that they'd never dared to say before. For the first few minutes people felt awkward but then it became stimulating and before long both groups were thoroughly enjoying themselves.

Then after 20 minutes we asked the two groups to swap positions and, based on what they'd heard, argue for the case they had just been opposing. Much to their surprise the two groups found that they were just as passionate as before.

This was the breakthrough moment. Suddenly Jenny's team understood the value of disagreement and were able to see that the power of challenge was not in being right or wrong but in surfacing information that would help them make the best possible decision. In essence this created the energy for a much bolder conversation.

If you want to promote healthy disagreement in your team then the essentials of building trust that we've talked about in Ignite are vital. It's also crucial to set up ground rules that encourage people to say what's on their mind and challenge each other. Only then will you develop the possibility mindset and open thinking that is so necessary for breakthrough.

Jenny did a great job in taking the team out of fear and into possibility. By encouraging creative conflict in her team she helped people to a new level of commitment, which has proved vital for the organisation and that has stimulated new and innovative ways of working.

Breaking the silence: how to make it work

Many people fear conflict. But imagine a world in which disagreement is fun!

1. Pick a long-standing elephant, taboo or inconvenient truth.
2. Invite disagreement. Split the team into two groups. Ask the groups to prepare arguments that justify opposing positions.
3. Encourage passion, straight talking and intentional listening and let the debate run for at least 20 minutes.
4. After 20 minutes ask the groups to switch sides and argue with as much passion for the view they previously opposed.
5. Initiate a conversation about the insights that emerged from the debate, what that might mean for the team and the best way forward. Look for curiosity, openness and alignment.
6. Choose a course of action that represents what has been spoken and directly tackles the issue.

Courageous conversations

Out beyond ideas of wrongdoing and rightdoing there is a field. I'll meet you there

Rumi

Whether seizing opportunities or tackling treacle, have no doubt that it will require you to step out of your comfort zone and have courageous conversations. This will mean being bold and having the courage to engage.

The word 'conversation' can of course feel passive – but that is not what we have in mind here. Courageous conversations require us to be vulnerable, unambiguous, fearless. They require as much listening as they do speaking and the intention of such conversations is to put reality on the table and fundamentally shift the issue.

If there is no difference made as a result of the conversation then either you have kept the conversation too safe or you haven't finished talking and listening to one another!

On one occasion we were working with a senior team that had serious goals, a culture to change and a workforce to engage. What became clear to us as the conversations started was there wasn't enough excitement in the room to charge a two-watt bulb. Deep treacle!

Sometimes the only way to expose such treacle is to tease people – so we asked whether anyone in the room felt even a tiny bit excited by the prospect of the transformation they were talking about leading. Did it leave them with their pulses racing and a bright light in their eye? Would they look forward to the next meeting on this subject?

Happily they smiled at this intervention because of course the opposite was true – an inconvenient truth had been revealed. The team felt they ought to be excited but they weren't. And it was only once they had admitted this that we were able to engage in the real conversation. What would help get them enthused? What would have to be possible for them to bring their energy to the change? What might personal success look like for them?

There is one especially powerful way to help teams that are stuck in this sort of treacle and that's to ask them what it would be like if they were really 'for' each other. We believe that everything can change when you are 'for' someone else and here's a piece of work that highlights its impact.

How to be 'for' someone

Everything is different when you are 'for' someone

Some conversations feel difficult as soon as you start to think about having them. You know the ones, where your energy drops and you start to think of ways around the issue. So how do you help people stop avoiding awkward topics and lean in to big conversations?

In Georgia's senior team, trust and relationships were poor. Honest conversations had stopped and the team had started fragmenting. Topics that needed to be talked through were avoided because they felt too difficult to tackle. The team had stopped being 'for' each other and the business was suffering because of it. Something had to change.

Faced with this scenario we asked the team to consider what being 'for' each other might look like.

- How do you behave and what do you believe when you are 'for' someone else?
- What do you need from your colleagues to feel that they are 'for' you?
- And what sort of impact does it make when people are 'for' one another?

Opening up this conversation gave Georgia's team new insights, both about exactly what it felt like in the team now and what might be possible. It was clear to everybody that they hadn't been 'for' each other for a long time. Everyone had more than one conversation they were avoiding. None of them could honestly say they were championing each other. And none of them were proud of it.

But to change this situation took courage. The team members would have to own their bad habits and look to repair damaged relationships. They would need to ask for help and invite a greater intimacy. They would need to speak and listen to one another with vulnerability. They would need to be 'for' each other.

To help the team take this step we asked everyone to face into the conversations that they needed to have and write an invitation to each of their colleagues as follows:

- Dear xxx. You are the person I most need to talk to
- What I would like to talk with you about is the following ...
- Why this is important to me is because...
- My intent and hope for this conversation is...

It seems like a simple enough structure but asking people to write down their invitations and then hand them out takes real commitment. And ensuring people were clear about what they wanted, and hoped for, helped them make it real.

The most critical piece here is to signal our positive intent. Without knowing this intent there are often misunderstandings. These conversations are courageous because they are designed to make a difference, the intent is to move us forward.

The joy of such an exercise is of course that people often have exactly the same invitations for one other. Both parties know exactly what conversations they need. And in the case of Georgia's team this was a watershed moment. There was relief and a dawning understanding that the power to make things different was in their own hands. Misunderstandings, distrust and old grievances were put aside.

The team spent time, talked and listened to one another and promises and requests were made. Sticky topics were aired as never before, but what was especially powerful was the stated desire from team members not to let such a situation arise again. They were determined to work on their differences and value one another's perspectives. And they committed to back each other to the hilt and go out of their way to build shared success.

CHOOSE NOW

Think of a conversation you avoided or kept too safe.

- What made you play it this way?
- What have you tolerated?
- What has been the impact on you and them of keeping the conversation small?

Now think of a courageous conversation you need to have.

- What will you need to say?
- How will you need to say it?
- What does being 'for' someone look like here?

IN SUMMARY

This chapter was about:

- Understanding the value of feedforward and how it can help you with your leadership impact
- Seizing opportunities through open goals, big bets and hidden treasure
- Tackling treacle by identifying elephants, taboos and inconvenient truths
- Having courageous conversations and being for someone else

Impact is about making such a difference that people can barely remember what it was like before you arrived. In the final chapter we will be looking at how you can sustain your energy and focus.

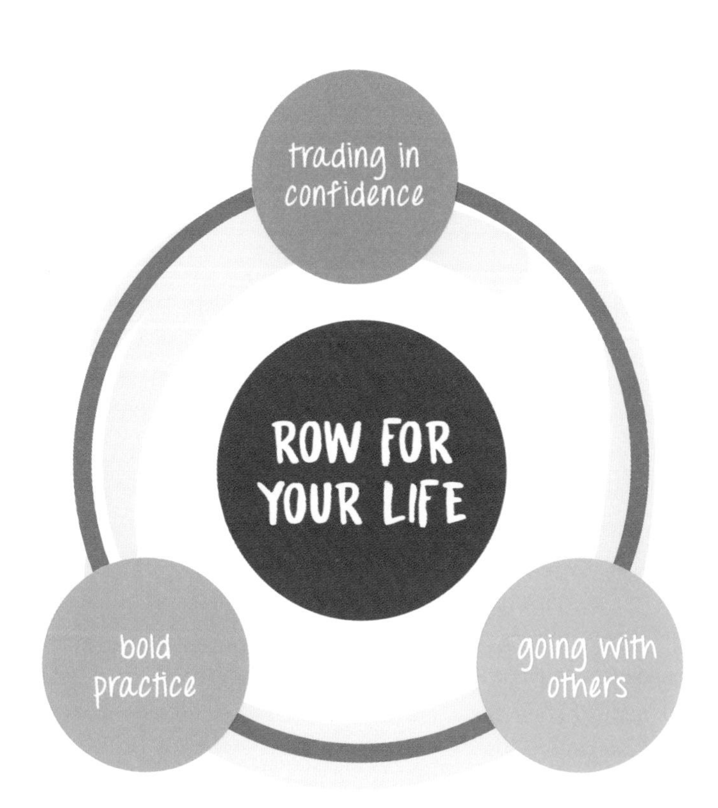
trading in confidence
ROW FOR YOUR LIFE
bold practice
going with others

Row for your life...

Hear the pounding of the waterfall, the roiling mist and energy, don't fear it. Row, row for your life toward it.

Mary Oliver

This final chapter is about how you take 4i Leadership and use it to make the difference to everything that matters most to you. In her fierce poem, West Wind#2, Mary Oliver demands that when we have heard in the distance something we can't ignore, we have to row for our life toward it.

This requires us to be 100% all-in; not sitting on the sidelines and watching the world go by, but being guided by that compelling drumbeat that perhaps only we can hear.

You will need ongoing and bolder conversations to sustain this. Such conversations will ensure you generate increasing levels of confidence and harness the energy and potential of the people you want to bring along with you. These bolder conversations will enable you to:

1. Instill more confidence
2. Create a sense of energy and possibility within your team
3. Embed continuous success through living practice

Trading in confidence

I am the greatest. I said that before I even knew I was!

Muhammad Ali

Essentially, as leaders, we are traders in confidence. Consider that in every interaction you have with someone else the intention should be to leave them feeling more confident. This applies whether your intention is to help, provoke, hold to account or set big challenges. The ability to fuel the confidence of those around you is priceless. Confident people are more energised, more focused, they are generally happier and more engaged. And crucially, confident people will look out for opportunities as well as being ready to challenge the treacle. They will bring energy and innovative thinking to all your endeavours as they pursue success.

Over the years we've been surprised how slow most leaders are in recognising the rocket fuel that comes when you fill people with confidence. Those that put confidence at the heart of their interactions inevitably create an uplifting sense of possibility. Make confidence your focus and you are guaranteed to generate sustained momentum.

When we first met Jasmin she told us how it was when she inherited her current team. What she found was a group of people who had everything needed by way of skill and experience but who had little belief in their ability to add value. Part of this low confidence could be attributed to the previous manager whose forceful approach had undermined any initiative or creative expression.

'I needed to ignite their belief' she said. 'So to start with I asked them to talk about those things they had done that made them feel proud. This took some patience – they were very reticent to start with – but eventually their stories started to emerge. And just talking about their past successes helped them to feel more positive and generated a new optimism.'

Jasmin then set about understanding the challenges the team were facing. Again it was clear that they were lacking belief. 'They were only thinking about the problem – their mindset was one of fear – they weren't bold enough to engage their imagination.' So she encouraged them to stretch themselves in team meetings and one-to-one conversations and constantly acknowledged them when she saw progress. And sure enough they started to stretch.

'It was great to see their belief returning and within a short time I saw their thinking and their work starting to make more impact. As a leader it's important both to encourage people and challenge them. The challenge is especially important when they believe something isn't possible. That's when you need to draw a line in the sand and say 'go again'. It's at these moments when people are asked to go beyond their self-imposed limitations that breakthroughs occur and confidence grows.'

Jasmin is a confidence builder by nature and her approach is contagious. 'I always help people see how they can be more successful. I help them understand where they are brilliant and where they need to grow. Everyone in my team knows where they stand in terms of performance and they all understand their role and how important they are to the whole team.'

Jasmin is also a results-focused leader and it's her belief that confidence fuels performance. And her team are delivering. Jasmin may be challenging to work for but her team would follow her anywhere. When we asked why they said 'because she encourages us to make our own decisions, she backs us and is always interested in our success – not just her success.'

Conversations for confidence

You can create more confidence in those around you by focusing on these critical conversations:

- Spend time talking about what people can be proud of. This will include their accomplishments, courageous moments and successes.
- Help them to think bigger. Don't accept mediocre solutions or small thinking. Encourage, explore and stretch them in order to reignite their hope and belief.
- Be clear on the value they bring and where they need to grow. Underline the positives in both these conversations. Celebrate their success and help them learn from failure.
- Bring meaning to what they are doing. Link all work and activity to the future you believe in and let people know how much they are contributing.

CHOOSE NOW

- Who around you needs an injection of belief?
- Start your next conversation with them with a clear intent about how you will fuel their confidence.

Going with others

If you want to go fast go alone. If you want to go far go with others

African proverb

Creating confidence is an essential practice for leaders. From here you can create more opportunities and make even more progress with the people you lead. When people work well together there is a sense of energy and possibility that creates momentum and embraces the challenges that arise. There is a feeling that all endeavours are productive, worthwhile and enjoyable.

Let us introduce you to Daniel, a director who, when we met him, wasn't thinking much about the energy that gets released when a team works brilliantly together. All he wanted was people to 'do their job'.

Daniel's CEO, however, believed that when you develop people then you improve performance and he asked us to pilot a workshop with Daniel focusing on high-impact teams.

Daniel went along with this initiative. He wasn't convinced about the focus on trust and personal conversation and didn't realise that there was hidden treasure to be found. However, when he asked his team for their feedback he realised that they had found it inspiring and really useful. So after his initial surprise at the impact this had, Daniel kept going.

What occurred over the next couple of years was one of the biggest team transformations that we have witnessed. Daniel had been schooled in the old way, believing that success could only be measured through regular reporting on hard measures. And yet these workshops were encouraging his people to go out of their way to help one another and this impacted powerfully on performance and results.

This was noticed and admired across the organisation and before he knew it Daniel, much to his delight and surprise, was soon seen as a leadership champion and someone who knew how to develop peak performance in teams.

From our work over the past 20 years we've taken everything we've seen and learnt about how people work best together and distilled it down to the following five principles. These are essential practices if you want to create a high impact team.

1. Teams move faster when they are personal

When teams only talk about project deadlines, sales targets and resource problems they typically have stressed, combative, fire-fighting conversations and a great deal of energy is spent in intellectual debate.

Daniel's team provided an illustration of what happens when teams get personal. They spent time listening to one another and found that they had much in common. This focus helped them build trust and support. They started to enjoy working together and brought shared belief and energy to their projects. With this new dynamic they were able to get through the everyday issues faster and spend more time focusing on how they could help each other with future projects.

2. Everyone succeeds when the team comes first

In many teams the focus on 'my job' and 'my area of responsibility' results in competing priorities and creates friction. The contrast in Daniel's team was that individual team members stopped thinking of their own role as being the most important part of their jobs and started thinking of their role in the team as being of primary importance. This showed up in them spending more time with each other and going out of their way to help each other succeed. They even started willingly giving away bits of their budget and offering resource to ensure that nobody had a shortfall.

3. Impact improves when you grow leadership capability

Teams often focus the majority of their time on fixing today's problems. With the positive shift in their own ways of working it soon became clear to Daniel and his team that they could make an even bigger impact by expanding their horizons. So they consciously started to develop leaders across the organisation and this made a big difference too. Soon it became clear that people were taking more ownership for their work. There was less passing of the buck and more proactivity. Importantly, this move towards empowerment was seen as being led collectively by Daniel's team. This helped provide a sense of connection and momentum that had previously been missing.

4. Opportunities open up when you are 'for' each other

Sometimes team members can get so busy and focused on their own targets and deadlines that they get siloed. In high-impact teams, however, the momentum gets sustained when people champion one another.

In Daniel's team, and across the organisation, this was encouraged through coaching, mentoring and a strong commitment to each other's success. Feedforward played a big part in this and the impact was tangible. When people believe wholeheartedly in their colleagues they go out of their way to help them succeed and create more opportunities. This doesn't mean creating more work – it means people helping each other to find and do more of the work they enjoy.

5. The culture comes alive when you acknowledge the people

We all know that celebrating success is important. But remember this isn't just about focusing on the results. Acknowledging the people, how they are working and what personal qualities they have brought that drive the success ... that's what people yearn for. They want to be seen, heard and recognised for their human qualities and when you celebrate these then you are building sustained performance. Teams are contagious entities and when you are in a great team you will see and feel the difference.

In Daniel's team they started to celebrate success and people felt proud of the progress they were making. Furthermore, survey results showed that in Daniel's division people were given real opportunities to succeed and engagement scores were high. This reputation fed directly into retention and recruitment as it became known that this wasn't a place where you had to 'watch your back' but rather a place where people have 'got your back'.

Keep the conversation going

The underpinning skill in all these conversations is to stay connected. And although this is a simple concept, it isn't easy. We yearn to be understood but we're often not vulnerable enough to allow others to help us.

Remember, most of the time, you won't get far – and it won't be as much fun – when you do things on your own. Most of us gain energy and thrive when we're engaged in something meaningful with others. At work we spend so much time with our colleagues that it's crazy not to want to feel that we're moving forward, failing and succeeding together.

So, when leading and working with others resist trying to problem-solve or come to conclusions too quickly. Instead remember to be curious. Ask the team to notice what they are tolerating that needs interrupting. Encourage them to imagine what could be better. Explore how ignition will make a difference and actively ask them to see where they need to focus in order to make a greater impact. This will build the two-way nature of sustaining conversations that creates the platform for peak performance.

CHOOSE NOW

- Take the five principles in this section and identify where your team is strong and where it needs to grow.
- Choose to ignite this conversation within your team.

Bold Practice

Remember that not getting what you want is sometimes a wonderful stroke of luck

Dalai Lama

It's our ability to practise that keeps us fresh and sustains our learning and growth. The moment we think we've got something right we tend to stop practising and when that happens 'watch out' – we fall into old habits and traps.

Practice helps us ensure that we pay attention to what's important and it allows us to learn from every project, relationship and experience.

As leaders we can also expect to encounter failure along the way, especially when we are practising something new or ground-breaking. The key message here is to embrace failure as an important part of bold practice. Sometimes we just make mistakes and fall flat on our face. At other times we realise that something's just not working or we're heading in the wrong direction. There is a way of dealing with this called 'fast failure' and here's the crux of it – expect it, recognise it, fail fast, learn from it and go again.

Fast failure

Fast failure stops us from getting hung up when it all goes wrong. Instead of withdrawing or pretending failure isn't happening, this approach ensures that we learn from our inevitable fallibility.

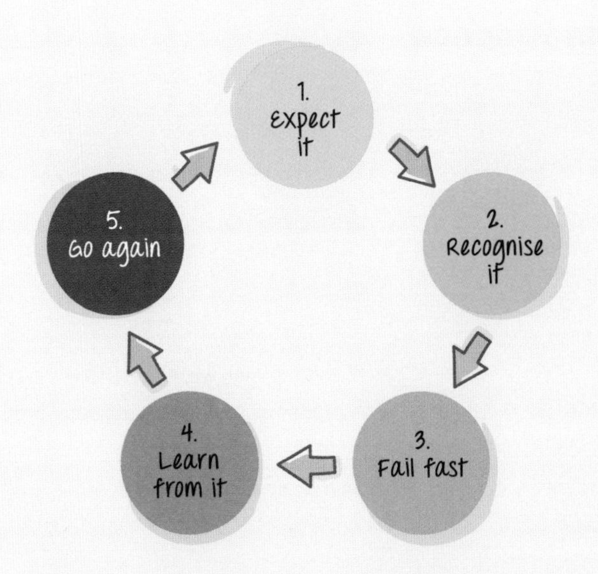

1. **Expect it** – this doesn't mean we should always expect to fail. Far from it, but we all experience failure at some point so be confident enough to know it will happen to you periodically and be ready to respond when it does.
2. **Recognise it** – our desire to avoid failure can make us blind to the thing that isn't working. But recognise it with consideration and compassion – think it through, because 'knee-jerk' reactions aren't helpful.
3. **Fail fast** – once you're clear something isn't working, stop it – be clear that you're stopping it and let people know.
4. **Learn from it** – with the help of others understand what was missing, why it didn't work and what you will take forward – use the experience to be better next time.
5. **Go again** –Take what you've learnt and get back in touch with your sense of possibility and go again – with joy in the learning, greater understanding and renewed enthusiasm.

Fast failure applies to all leadership practice and to just about anything else we are attempting in our lives. When we are trying to make big changes the pressure to get it right can be enormous and is often impossible to achieve. Getting it wrong is an integral part of learning. It's also a sign that you're dancing along that edge where creativity and possibility are at their most potent. It's the place where the risk of failure can be at its highest. But you're occupying that space because the joy of the journey and the difference it could make feels enlivening and worthwhile.

In many work cultures people spend much of their time trying to avoid failure but when you accept the idea of bold practice then there is no failure, only learning. And because we're all imperfect you'll probably notice that you also still have some learning left to do. So, hold your practice lightly and remember to smile at yourself when you are experiencing the downturns as well as when you are enjoying those heady moments of success.

Choose to practise

The following three pages provide a framework to help you start practising 4i Leadership. Use it on your own to help you think about your leadership or use it with others to start a bolder conversation.

4i Leadership
The essential guide to your practice

Paying attention to your leadership practice will help you grow faster and make more impact. On the following pages we have summarised everything in this book so that you can remind yourself of the opportunities that exist for bolder conversations. Here are some essential principles to keep in mind as you choose what and how to practise:

- Choose to practise something that will make a significant difference to you or others
- Be authentic. In other words don't suddenly try to become someone you are not. Rather, become the most powerful version of yourself that you can be
- Tell other people what you are practising so that they know how you are looking to grow and can help you build your confidence
- Don't expect to get it right first time. But be persistent and see how fast you learn
- Notice when you have made progress and don't rush past it. Find a way to acknowledge your success as it arrives
- And as part of all of the above remember to invite people you trust to support you. Enrol coaches, colleagues, direct reports, friends and family so that they consistently give you the ruthless support you will need to succeed

4i Leadership
The essential guide to your practice

1. **Start a bolder conversation** – be couragous

- Choose your mindset – get in touch with your sense of possibility and be ready to notice your 1st 2nd and 3rd thoughts
- Get clear on how you bring the energies to life and how you bring creativity to them
- Start a conversation that matters

2. **Interrupt** – you get what you tolerate

- Where can you see the need for a wake-up call?
- What are you tolerating?
- What are the facts and stories around what needs interrupting?
- What compelling interruption do you need to make?

3. **Imagine** – dare to dream

- Remind yourself of your leadership map – what you stand for and what you're here for and how you want to lead...
- What can you imagine that is better and creates more possibility and energy?
- What matters most to you about this?
- Who will you share this with?

4. **Ignite** – bring others with you

- Who do you need to ignite and bring with you to start making more of a difference?
- Where can you forge more trust to help with this?
- How can you make an irresistible invitation to them?
- What idea, if it spread like wildfire, would change everything?

5. **Impact** – make it happen

- Where are you going to commit to action?
- What is your impact intended?
- What are the opportunities you want to seize?
- Where is there treacle that you need to tackle?
- What are the courageous conversations you'll need to have?

6. **Row for your life** – keep it going

- Spend time creating confidence in those around you
- Look at the teams you're working with – create an environment that ensures they are able to work brilliantly together
- Know that you're practising and learn from the failures and successes

Afterword

Thank you for reading *4i Leadership*. The final inspiration and encouragement we would like to leave you with is to think about what bolder conversations you need to pursue.

Take any of the perspectives you've read about in this book and open up new and important conversations. This is what we believe starts to make a difference and whilst we are delighted that you've bought this book, don't just keep it on your shelf – it will make much more of a difference to you if you use it.

So finally, be inspired by possibility...

Start a bolder conversation.
Leadership is personal.
Notice what you are tolerating
And practise interruption.
Hold it lightly.
Be playful
And don't fear failure.
Be vulnerable,
Invite support and
Find hope and joy
In every interaction.

Use your leadership map.
Bring your energy and choose
Your mindset.
Dare to dream

Be brave and purposeful
And join up with others.
Stand for something!
Bring conviction,
Find your spark
And always forge trust.

Tackle treacle and
Seize opportunities
And make the impact you intend.
Trade in confidence and
Go with others.
Don't fear failure.
Believe in what's possible!
Hear the pounding of the waterfall,
The roiling mist and energy,
Don't fear it.
Row, row for your life toward it.

Additional notes

Start a bolder conversation – additional notes

Choosing the right conversation

What conversations ignite possibility? Here are three different but typical conversations that can help you identify the ways in which you interact.

Conversation 1. The 'pleasantries' conversation

This is the conversation you have when you've met someone and you ask them 'how are you?' or 'what are you up to today' but you don't expect or want an answer. The polite response you get, is 'I'm fine' or 'I'm really busy' or perhaps 'still here!'. Occasionally you will get a reply from more upbeat people of 'really good' or 'feeling brilliant'.

Pleasantry conversations are hygiene conversations designed to do nothing more than maintain the status quo. In this respect they aren't really conversations at all, they are simply tail-wagging mechanisms that allow us to pass on by.

Conversation 2. The 'project' conversation

This is a more substantial conversation and in work such conversations are omnipresent. The context here is task and action and from a work perspective that makes them easy and expected. 'What's the agenda?' 'What have you got on?' 'What progress are you making?'

These are the kind of conversations that focus on a problem and allow us to get on with our activity. But notice that these conversations typically have a focus on structure, process or timing. They demand answers and facts. And in this respect the two-way nature of these conversations is severely limited. They might bring clarity but they are seldom inviting or engaging.

Conversation 3. The 'personal' conversation

Personal conversations occur when you ask people how they are and you really want them to tell you. You give them time to answer. You are interested, present and receptive.

Vicki is a leader who simply can't imagine not bringing this conversation to her work. She has a keen interest in knowing how her team are doing so that she can support them properly. She brings a vitality to her encounters because of her engagement with others. And because of this attitude she has a team where people go out of their way for each other.

People who have this conversation bring an intention to their relationships. They are thoughtful and provide space to others. In this conversation there is as much listening as there is talking. And because people feel they are in it together such conversations help to release ideas, energy and performance.

CHOOSE NOW

- Think of three key people you work with and remember your last conversation with them. What type of conversation was it? Next time you meet choose to make it more personal.

Interrupt – additional notes

It all starts with noticing

Questions are a great way to start noticing what isn't working and what, therefore, you might need to interrupt. Here are a series of questions for you, for your team and for your organisation to get you started.

It can be useful to talk these questions through with someone who supports you and wants you to be a stronger leader in all areas of your life. This might be a coach, someone at work who really gets you or even a good friend. Try inviting them to help think through your answers to these questions.

Your personal leadership

- What are you tolerating in your life/work?
- Where in your life/work are you feeling uninspired?
- In what relationships do you make no effort?
- If you had one leadership ability that would transform your life/work what would it be? And what does that tell you about what needs interrupting?
- Where and in what ways are you being brilliant?

Your team leadership

- If you had to score your team out of 10 what would you give them? Is that score good enough?
- With whom are you accepting 'average' because it feels too tough to do anything about it?
- What really slows your team down?
- What in your team is really annoying?
- What are you most proud of in your team and do you regularly tell them so?

Your organisational leadership

- What aspects of your organisational culture take it forward and what aspects slow it down?
- What is really difficult to talk about?
- What would you change tomorrow about the organisation that would transform the ability to deliver outstanding results?
- What are the questions for you that refuse to go away?
- What is it about your leadership that contributes to this?

Imagine – additional notes

Ignite your imagination

Instead of wondering when your next holiday is, maybe you should set up a life you don't need to escape – Seth Godin

---

We can access our imagination in many different ways. Some people just need to pause and get in the right frame of mind and dreams appear. Others need more of a prompt.

Possibility thinking

When you want to build a sense of possibility ask yourself the following questions

- What could you imagine doing that would be more exciting, more effective, fun, joyful, better, fulfilling, purposeful?
- If you didn't need the job you are in now then what different choices might you be making?
- Imagine you woke up tomorrow and a breakthrough had occurred in your life. What would be different?

Clarify what you want!

You might have a dream but remember to get tangible – exactly what do you want? Don't let realism get in your way here!

- What does wild success look like?
- If you were unstoppable how soon would results start to appear?
- Who would you like to accompany you on your journey?
- What does a first brave step look like?

Access your inspiration

Inspiration can feel like a high bar but perhaps it's not as far away as you think.

- Who inspires you? What is it they do? How can you model yourself on them?
- What activities raise your spirits or fill you with energy and optimism? How can you do more of them?
- Think of an experience in the past when you were 'in the zone'. How did you get into that state? What might you need to do to get there again?

An exercise in creativity

A few years ago we introduced an exercise, inspired by Sir Ken Robinson, to help people get back in touch with a part of themselves that they may have forgotten. We asked the group we were working with to divide into two and spend some time thinking about what they would do if they were suddenly given a free day with no access to work or the internet.

Both groups headed off for a 20-minute conversation but we asked one group to approach the exercise as if they were seven years old.

When they returned, the first group had a great list involving DIY jobs, walking, exercising, reading and entertaining themselves. The second group, however, were building camps, engaging in mock battles, flying to the moon, fighting dragons and building rope swings.

Of course many of us at seven years old have no limits to our imagination. We don't care if it's impossible and we dream in any way we want. And that's the point. Realism can seriously constrain us.

What we need to learn, if we want to release our imagination, is to find again that part in us where anything feels possible.

Ignite – additional notes

Practising deep trust

You have to keep breaking your heart until it opens – Rumi

A while ago we came across an experiment that was designed to see if people could fall in love on their first ever meeting. They were given 36 questions to answer together and the impact of this experiment on the participants was profound. We wondered if an adapted version could help people at work ignite trust and possibility in their relationships. So far the results have been staggering so we've included them here. Sit down with someone you work with and have a go.

- What would be a perfect work day for you?
- What excites you about leading at work?
- What do you care about regarding the future of your organisation?
- What is it about work you feel most grateful for?
- If you could wake up tomorrow having gained one leadership quality or ability, what would it be?
- What is the greatest accomplishment of your working life?
- Name three things you appear to have in common.
- What do you value most in work colleagues?
- Share three positive characteristics that you've already noticed in your partner.
- For you to have a successful relationship with your colleague what is important for them to know?
- Share a problem you have at work – ask for their help with it.

Collaboration

Collaboration cannot be forced; people only collaborate if they are willing to do so. It arises as one of the key benefits of building trusting relationships. Here are some reminders of how to initiate, cement and sustain collaboration

1. Initiate collaboration by:

- **a)** building trusting relationships where people find out more about what each other cares about and what each other wants.
- **b)** looking for opportunities that are clearly based on win-win outcomes.

2. Cement collaboration by:

- **a)** bringing interest, care and positive intention into your relationships.
- **b)** going out of your way to share resources, information and energy.

3. Sustain collaboration by:

- **a)** following through on the relationship – not just the project. Acknowledge them for everything they brought to the venture.
- **b)** looking out for further opportunities that support the ambition or dream of the other party.

Impact – additional notes

Clarity and courageous conversations

Clarity is kind. If we aren't clear about what we are asking of people then we are not helping them in any way. This is why courageous conversations are so important for leaders and followers alike. They remove uncertainty and doubt. Here are the key ingredients of such conversations:

- They are underpinned by their focus. Courageous conversations bring into the light something that has previously been hidden.
- They are heartfelt. In this sense they are both important and they are imbued with care and consideration. This is a conversation based on desire for deeper relationship.
- They are straight talking. In these conversations we dare to say things that need to be said. This may make the conversations uncomfortable but it can also make them revelatory.
- They are unambiguous. These conversations leave others in no doubt about what is at stake and what may need to change.
- They are two-way. Courageous conversations invite enquiry and dialogue. They require vulnerability and generosity.

How to start a courageous conversation

Here are some real examples of people who invited their colleagues to have a courageous conversation that addressed the opportunities and/or tackled the treacle they were facing. These written invitations were based on what the conversation was about, why it was seen as necessary and what the intent was in having it.

Dear John,

- *I would like a conversation with you* about *the way we interact in our meetings.*
- *I would like this conversation* because *I notice that we are often at odds and rarely listen to each other. This is getting in the way of the great project we are working on.*
- *My* intent *is to understand more about what you want, how we can use our combined experience to make a real difference and grow our relationship so that we both feel valued and heard.*

I'm really looking forward to talking this through with you.

Dear Esme,

- *I would like a conversation with you* about *a new opportunity I have seen for us.*
- *I would like this conversation with you* because *it's not something we usually do and I think it will be really exciting.*
- *My* intent *is to start a conversation where I share my idea and we explore it together.*

Let me know when you are available to talk this through.

Dear Ali,

- *I would like a conversation with you* about *your leadership.*
- *I would like this conversation with you* because *I am noticing that you are spending a lot of time telling me what to do when I don't think you need to.*
- *My* intent *is to understand what you need, how I can help and also how I can work brilliantly with your support.*

I'm really looking forward to working this out with you.

How can you create a life that is truly extraordinary?

What would be possible if you could?

Put aside all your preconceptions about personal development. Ian Lock's ***Being Extraordinary*** isn't just an important read, it's a big conversation with a trusted friend, sharing experiences and insights, asking challenging questions, and pushing you to reach further, explore deeper and achieve more.

The ambition here is no less than to have you 'own and live the life you want'. So be prepared to be provoked and challenged, and get ready to shift your thinking and belief.

Recognised as a brilliant coach and consultant, Ian Lock is a guide you can trust. Let him take you on an exploration into what matters to you and how you can get more of what you care about.

ISBN 978-1-5272-4848-9
Format Paperback/Kindle
Available on Amazon

www.being-extraordinary.com

Index